THE REPRESENTATIVE INHERITORS OF THE PROVINCIAL INTANGIBLE CULTURAL HERITAGE PROJECTS OF SHANDONG PROVINCE

山东省省级非物质文化遗产项目代表性传承人

第四卷

（Volume Ⅳ）

李国琳　主编

山东大学出版社

《山东省省级非物质文化遗产项目代表性传承人》
编 辑 委 员 会

Editorial Board of *The Representative Inheritors of the Provincial Intangible Cultural Heritage Projects of Shandong Province*

序

传承人是历史文化的重要承载者和传递者，他们身上承载着丰富知识、精湛技艺、实践经验等重要内容，是非物质文化遗产活态传承的重要组成部分，关乎每个项目是否能够长久流传于世。因此，保护、宣传、扶持传承人对于进一步做好非物质文化遗产（简称“非遗”）的保护工作具有重要意义。

山东是孔孟之乡、礼仪之邦，经过千百年的历史进程，形成了凝聚着齐鲁儿女勤劳与智慧的非物质文化遗产。近年来，全省各级文化主管部门认真贯彻中央和省委有关部署和要求，积极推动非遗的创造性转化和创新性发展，形成了非遗保护的“山东模式”，涌现了非遗名录山东现象、非遗传承山东路径、非遗培训山东探索、非遗利用山东实践等一大批具有浓郁山东特色的非遗保护传承做法和经验，整体工作走在全国前列。目前，山东省共有联合国教科文组织认定的“人类非遗代表作名录”项目8项、国家级代表性名录项目173项、省级代表性名录项目751项、市级代表性名录项目3490项、县级代表性名录项目10544项。现有国家级代表性传承人94名、省级代表性传承人447名、市级代表性传承人2312名、县级代表性传承人6717名。编撰《山东省省级非物质文化遗产项目代表性传承人》的目的，是希望通过此书，向民众介绍山东省国家级、省级传承人的基本情况、技艺特征、授徒传承等内容，展现山东省非遗传承人的精神风貌，增强民众对山东省传承人的了解，使得本书成果惠及大众，为社会共享。

非物质文化遗产是一个民族的生命记忆，体现着民族的智慧和精神。做好传承人的记录工作，就是在保护中华传统文化的基因，为中华文明接续薪火，也是为后人研究、宣传、利用非物质文化遗产提供宝贵资料。新时代，新担当，新作为，山东非遗保护工作将以习近平新时代中国特色社会主义思想为指导，不断推动全省非遗保护工作继续走在全国前列，为实现中华民族伟大复兴的中国梦而贡献更大的力量。

（山东省文化和旅游厅党组书记、厅长，山东省文物局局长　王磊）

PREFACE

Inheritors are important carriers and transmitters of history and culture. They have rich knowledge, exquisite skills and practical experience, etc. They are an important part of the active inheritance of intangible cultural heritage, and they are of vital importance to each project in terms of durability and propagation. Therefore, it is of great significance to protect, publicize and support the inheritors for the further protection of intangible cultural heritage.

Shandong Province is the hometown of Confucius and Mencius and the state of etiquette. After thousands of years of history, it has formed its intangible cultural heritage that embodies the diligence and wisdom of Qilu people. In recent years, the competent cultural authorities at all levels in Shandong Province have seriously implemented the relevant arrangements and requirements of the Central Committee and the Provincial Committee. They actively promoted the creative transformation and innovative development of intangible cultural heritage, and formed a "Shandong Model" of intangible cultural heritage protection. A large number of rich Shandong characteristics emerged, such as Shandong phenomenon of intangible cultural heritage list, Shandong path of intangible cultural heritage inheritance, Shandong exploration of intangible cultural heritage training, and Shandong practice of intangible cultural heritage utilization. The overall work is at the forefront of the country. At present, Shandong Province has 8 items in the "list of representative works of human intangible cultural heritage" recognized by UNESCO, 173 items in the national representative list, 751 items in the provincial representative list, 3,490 items in the municipal representative list and 10,544 items in the county-level representative list. There are 94 national, 447 provincial, 2,312 municipal and 6,717 county-level representative inheritors in Shandong Province. The purpose of compiling *The Representative Inheritors of The Provincial Intangible Cultural Heritage Projects of Shandong Province* is to introduce the basic information, technical characteristics, apprenticeship and other aspects of national and provincial inheritors to the public, show the spirit of Shandong Province's inheritors, and familiarize the public with Shandong Province's inheritors. We hope that the fruit of this book will benefit the public and be shared by the society.

Intangible cultural heritage is the life memory of a nation, which embodies the wisdom and spirit of the nation. Make a record of the work of inheritors is to protect the genes of Chinese traditional culture, to continue the Chinese civilization, and to provide valuable information for future generations to study, publicize and use intangible cultural heritage. A new era asks for new responsibilities and new actions. The protection of intangible cultural heritage in Shandong Province will be guided by Xi Jinping's Thought on Socialism with Chinese Characteristics for a New Era. We will continue to push the province's intangible cultural heritage protection work ahead of the rest of the country and make greater contributions to the realization of the Chinese dream of the great rejuvenation of the Chinese nation.

(Wang Lei, secretary of the party group and director of the Department of Culture and Tourism of Shandong Province, director of Shandong Provincial Bureau of Cultural Relics)

目 录 CONTENTS >>>

民间文学
Folk Literature

传统音乐
Traditional Music

传统舞蹈
Traditional Dance

传统戏剧
Traditional Drama

曲艺
Folk Art Forms

传统体育、游艺与杂技
Traditional Sports, Entertainment and Acrobatics

传统美术 Traditional Arts

传统技艺 Traditional Artistry

山东省省级非物质文化遗产项目
代表性传承人

第四卷

民间文学

Folk Literature

柳毅传说传承人——张宝辉

张宝辉，男，1955 年出生，山东潍坊人，山东省民俗学会理事。

自唐朝始，柳毅传说就在民间广泛流传，根据这一民间传说，唐朝李朝威写有文言小说《柳毅传》，元朝尚仲贤写有杂剧《柳毅传书》。潍坊柳毅传说有两大特点：一是作家文学作品中的柳毅与当地柳氏家族的先祖柳毅叠合在一起，在神话祖先的过程中形成了家族内部的信仰；二是出于当时生产力低下和生产生活的需要，在民间逐渐演变为广泛的民间信仰。

生活在柳毅传说之乡的张宝辉儿时在脑海中就装满了“柳毅传说”的民间传奇故事。20 世纪 90 年代，张宝辉分管宗教管理工作，他通过这一途径与许多民俗信众接触，获得了大量的第一手资料。2002 年，因被调到区政协从事文史工作，他又从调查、挖掘、研究的角度，系统地梳理了“柳毅传说”的故事内容。

张宝辉不但能从理论上阐明中国文学史上“柳毅传书”与在地化的“柳毅传说”的内在传承关系，而且还能够完整地口述或用文字表述在地化的“柳毅传说”的全部内容。此外，他还对“柳毅传说”的文化分布地域、活态的文化传承濒危状态及其固化的文化遗产存在情况等有较为全面的了解。

多年来，张宝辉为柳毅传说的传承做了大量工作。2008 年，他邀请全国知名民俗学者，组织召开了柳毅山文化学术研讨会，会后结集出版了《柳毅山文集》。他还完成了《国家级非物质文化遗产——柳毅传说》一书的初稿。寒亭区成立“柳毅山文化研究会”后，张宝辉在继续对“柳毅传说”进行深度研究的同时，还多批次带领山东大学民俗学的硕、博士研究生前往柳毅山，进行田野调查，帮助他们完成学术论文的撰写。

Zhang Baohui—Inheritor of Liu Yi's Legends

Zhang Baohui, male, was born in Weifang City, Shandong Province in 1955. He is the director of Shandong Folklore Society.

Since the Tang Dynasty, Liu Yi's Legends have been widely spread among the people. According to the legend, Li Chaowei of the Tang Dynasty wrote the classical Chinese novel *Liu Yi's Biography* and Shang Zhongxian of the Yuan Dynasty wrote the opera *Liu Yi's Biography*. Liu Yi's Legends in Weifang have two main features: one is that Liu Yi in the writers' literary works overlaps with Liu Yi, the ancestor of the local Liu family, forming the belief within the family in the process of deifying the ancestor; the other is that because of the low productivity and the need of production and life at that time, it gradually evolved into a folk belief among the people.

Zhang Baohui, who lived in the hometown of Liu Yi's Legends, had been filled with Liu Yi's Legends in mind since his childhood. In the 1990s, Zhang Baohui was in charge of religious management. During the work, he got in touch with many folk believers and obtained a lot of first-hand information. In 2002, because he was transferred to the District CPPCC to engage in literary and historical work, he systematically combed Liu Yi's Legends from the perspective of investigation and research.

Zhang Baohui is not only able to theoretically clarify the inherent relationship between Liu Yi's Biography in the history of Chinese literature and localized Liu Yi's Legends, but also can fully express the whole content of the localized Liu Yi's Legends orally or literally. In addition, he also has a comprehensive understanding of the cultural distribution of Liu Yi's Legends, the endangered state of the living cultural inheritance, and the existence of the solidified cultural heritage.

Over the years, Zhang Baohui has done a lot of work for the inheritance of Liu Yi's Legends. In 2008, he invited well-known folklore scholars from all over the country to convene an academic seminar on Liuyishan Culture. After the seminar, he compiled and published the *Liuyishan Collected Works*. He also completed the first draft of *Liu Yi's Biography, a National Intangible Cultural Heritage*. After the establishment of the Liuyishan Cultural Center in Hanting District, Zhang Baohui continued his in-depth study of the Liu Yi's Legends, and led many batches of postgraduate and doctoral students majoring folklore in Shandong University to Liuyishan, to conduct field surveys, and help them complete their academic papers.

蒙山传说传承人——张莉

张莉，女，1975 年出生，山东蒙阴人。

蒙山悠久的历史和雄险奇秀的景色形成了历代传诵的美丽、丰富、曲折、动人的蒙山传说。现流传的各类传说故事共计 130 余篇，有《孙三爷庙》《张茂申》《倒霉的姜太公》《懂鸟语的人公冶长》《麻妮》等人物传说、《乾与坤》《大禹和女娇》等神话故事、《缘为媒》《王小儿与活画》《穷八辈告命》《大妮二妮烙皮狐》等生活故事。蒙山传说是劳动群众表达自己真情实感的一种方式，歌颂了沂蒙人民勤劳、淳朴、勇敢、智慧的高贵品质。

张莉出生于书香之家，并在良好的家庭氛围的熏陶下形成了热爱文化的优秀品格。1997 年 12 月，张莉进入蒙阴县文化馆工作。在长期的工作实践中，她多次深入地方搜集资料，并数次采访了李因星老人，将大量遗落民间的蒙山传说的精粹集结整理。2011 年以来，张莉收集整理了蒙山传说故事 20 多篇，并将所有的作品结集出版。

为了让蒙山传说这一可贵的精神财富充分发挥其价值，张莉将蒙山传说的部分故事改成画册出版，使其不仅作为普通老百姓日常口头交流的传说知识，更成为蒙阴甚至山东人民教育、启迪后人的教材，从而使蒙山传说能够在历史宝库中源远流长、经久不息。

近年来，张莉编纂的故事集《蒙山的传说》获山东省第九届民俗学优秀成果二等奖。她还整理出版了包括蒙山传说在内的《蒙阴县非物质文化遗产普查资料汇编》和《蒙阴县非物质文化遗产线索实物登记表》等系列丛书，为蒙山传说的传承与发展做出了重要贡献。

Zhang Li—Inheritor of Mengshan Legends

Zhang Li, female, was born in Mengyin County, Shandong Province in 1975.

The long history of Mount Meng and its magnificent scenery have formed the beautiful, rich, intricate and moving legends that have been passed down from generation to generation. There are more than 130 legendary stories, such as "Temple of Sun Sanye" "Zhang Maoshen" "Bad-luck Jiang Taigong" "Gong Ye Chang People Who Understands Bird Language" "Ma Ni", fairy tales such as "Heaven and Earth" "Da Yu and Nüjiao", life stories such as "Destiny as Matchmaker""Wang Xiaoer and Living Pictures" "Fate of the Eight Poor Generations" and "Da Ni, and Er Ni Burn Fox", and so on. Mengshan Legends is a way for the working people to express their true feelings, which eulogizes the noble qualities of the Yimeng people, such as diligence, simplicity, fearlessness and smartness.

Zhang Li was born in a family of scholars, and she has formed an excellent character of loving culture under the influence of the inspiring family atmosphere. In December 1997, Zhang Li started to work at the Mengyin Cultural Center. During her long-term work practice, she has repeatedly collected information from locals, and interviewed the elderly Li Yinxing several times, gathered and sorted out the essence of a large number of Mengshan Legends which scattered in the folk. Since 2011, Zhang Li has collected more than 20 stories of Mengshan Legends and published all the works.

In order to give full play to the valuable spiritual wealth of Mengshan Legends, Zhang Li changed some stories of Mengshan Legends into picture albums for publication, making them not only the legendary knowledge of daily oral communication among ordinary people, but also the textbook of education, enlightenment and inspiration for the people in Mengyin and even Shandong Province, thus enabling Mengshan Legends to have a long and lasting history.

In recent years, Zhang Li's collection of stories, *The Mengshan Legends*, won the second prize of the 9th Folklore Outstanding Achievement Award of Shandong Province. She also compiled and published a series of books, including *The Collection of Intangible Cultural Heritage in Meng Yin County* and *The Physical Registration Form of Intangible Cultural Heritage Clues in Mengyin County*, which made an important contribution to the inheritance and development of the Mengshan Legends.

胡峄阳传说传承人——胡孝华

胡孝华，男，1961 年出生，山东青岛人。

胡峄阳传说起源于清康熙年间，根植于胶东半岛千百年来的历史文化之中，内容丰富，历史悠久，影响范围广，具有极高的民俗学价值和文学艺术价值。胡峄阳传说故事共 104 篇，主要内容为胡峄阳帮穷扶贫、济世救人、扶正祛邪、劝人向善、扬善惩恶、义感生灵、诲人不倦、教书育人、生有异禀、吉人天相等。

从 6 岁时起，胡孝华每逢年节就随父亲到胡峄阳祠堂叩拜并聆听胡峄阳传说。成年后，他仍不断搜集、整理各种胡峄阳传说的相关资料，为传承、发展胡峄阳传说奠定了坚实的基础。

胡孝华勤于研究、不断探索，在继承历代胡峄阳传说传承人总结的能谋善断、料事如神等九大特点之上，他把胡峄阳传说所涉及的题材归纳为五大类：一是风物类，14 篇；二是动物、植物类，6 篇；三是民俗类，3 篇；四是神话类，52 篇；五是生活类，29 篇。他还把近几年收集到的传说整理成文字，对一些内容大致相同但说法不一的“不同版本”进行记录和存档。

胡孝华常年参与搜集、整理胡峄阳事迹和传说，于 2007 年出版胡峄阳遗著《柳溪碎语》《易象授蒙》《竹庐家聒》《友义》《松轩九图》等，编印《胡峄阳传说》第一集、第二集；由胡孝华主持成立峄阳柳腔剧团，将国家级非遗项目柳腔与胡峄阳传说进行有机结合。其中，剧团编演的柳腔《胡影寻父》《胡峄阳求学》被评为“青岛市非物质文化遗产保护工作亮点项目”。他整理的峄阳古曲《梧桐秋月》获青岛市委宣传部、城阳区政府举办的民族乐器比赛一等奖。2012 年，他组织开展胡峄阳传说进课堂活动，使胡峄阳传说在中小学生中得到传承。他还多次主持召开胡峄阳传说和胡峄阳文化研究会，大力宣传胡峄阳传说。

Hu Xiaohua—
Inheritor of Hu Yiyang's Legends

Hu Xiaohua, male, was born in Qingdao City, Shandong Province in 1961.

Hu Yiyang's Legends originated in the reign of Emperor Kangxi in the Qing Dynasty and rooted in the history and culture of Jiaodong Peninsula for thousands of years. It has rich content, long history and a wide range of influence. It has very high folklore value and literary and artistic value. There are a total of 104 legendary stories about Hu Yiyang, which mainly include helping the poor, saving the world, strengthening justice and eliminating the evil, persuading people to do good deeds, promoting the kind and punishing the evil, inspiring the living creatures with righteousness, persuading people to be devoted to teaching and educating, born with gifts, and always being a lucky fellow, and etc.

When he was only six years old, Hu Xiaohua followed his father to worship Hu Yiyang memorial temple and listen to Hu Yiyang's Legends during the Spring Festival holidays every year. As a grown-up, he continued to collect and sort out all kinds of relevant materials of Hu Yiyang's Legends, which laid a solid foundation for the inheritance and development of Hu Yiyang's Legends.

Hu Xiaohua is diligent in research and constant exploration. On the basis of inheriting the nine characteristics summarized by the successors of Hu Fuyang's legends, such as resourcefulness, foretelling things with miraculous accuracy, he classifies the subjects involved in Hu Fuyang's legends into five categories: 14 articles about scenery; 6 articles about animals and plants; 3 articles about folklore; 52 articles about myth; and 29 articles about life. He also collated the legends collected in recent years into texts, and recorded and archived "different versions" with similar contents but different opinions.

Hu Xiaohua is involved in collecting and sorting out Hu Xiaoyang's deeds and legends all the year round. In 2007, he published Hu's legacy works *Liuxi Suiyu, Yixiang Shoumeng, Zhulu Jiaguo*, *You Yi, Nine Pictures of Songxuan,* and compiled and printed Volumes 1 and 2 of *Hu Yiyang's Legends.* Hu Xiaohua presided over the establishment of the Liuqiang Opera Troupe in Yiyang, which organically combines Liuqiang Opera, the national intangible culture heritage project with Hu Yiyang's legends. Among them, Liuqiang Opera *Hu Ying Looking for Father* and *Hu Yiyang Pursuing Study* compiled by the troupe won the highlight project of intangible cultural heritage protection in Qingdao City; the reorganized ancient song *Wutong Qiuyue* won the first prize in the national musical instrument competition held by the Propaganda Department of Qingdao Municipal Committee and Chengyang District Government; in 2012, he organized "Hu Yiyang's Legends Entering Classroom", so that Hu Yiyang's legends were passed down among primary and middle school students. He also hosted seminars on Hu Yiyang's legends and Hu Yiyang culture several times, vigorously publicizing Hu Yiyang's legends.

李左车传说传承人——邹学顺

邹学顺，男，1948 年出生，山东安丘人。

据《雹泉李氏族谱原续》记载，李左车，安丘雹泉人，秦汉之际名士。李左车传说起源于秦汉时期，世代不绝，流传于山东、河北、安徽一带。其内容大致可分为两类：一类是在《史记》《聊斋志异》等经典著作中关于李左车军事思想及传奇事迹的记载。另一类是民间流传的关于他悲天悯人的高尚品德以及作为“雹神”化身的传奇故事。李左车传说内容丰富多彩，情节夸张，充满想象，涵盖民众对历史的认识、评价及由此产生的爱憎之情，具有较高的文学、民俗价值。6 月 27 日是“雹神爷”李左车的生日，每到这时当地民众都会自发地组织以纪念李左车为主题的活动，以此弘扬他惩恶扬善、施惠于民的精神。

邹学顺国学功底深厚，长期从事李左车传说的搜集、整理与研究工作，热心传播民俗文化。他多次发起倡议，并慷慨解囊投资建设李左车纪念馆，长期的学习和研究为发展、传承李左车传说奠定了坚实的基础。

邹学顺多采用通俗易懂的艺术手法，以讲故事的形式讲述李左车传说，通过积极向上的故事和发人深省的教诲，引导人们培养勤于动脑的创造精神、惩恶扬善的正义精神、悲天悯人的人道精神和崇尚气节的爱国精神，起到加强品德修养、提升人文素养的作用。

2012 年，邹学顺荣获第二届中国“非遗”博览会传承人展示奖。多年来，他努力探索、善于钻研、积极奉献，通过李左车纪念馆向群众宣传李左车传说，收藏有关李左车传说的画册、马槽、天台柱等资料及实物，筹资建设李左车雕塑铜像，为后人研究李左车传说提供了宝贵的历史资料。

Zou Xueshun—
Inheritor of Li Zuoju's Legends

Zou Xueshun, male, was born in Anqiu, Shandong Province in 1948.

According to the *Original Continuation of Baoquan Li's Family Pedigree*, Li Zuoju, born in Baoquan Town, Anqiu Country, was a famous scholar in the Qin and Han Dynasties. Li Zuoju's Legends originated in the Qin and Han Dynasties and have been passed down for generations in Shandong, Hebei and Anhui provinces. The content can be roughly divided into two categories: One is the record of Li Zuoju's military thoughts and legendary deeds in classical works such as *Records of the Grand Historian of China, Strange Tales from Make-do Studio.* The other is the legendary stories about his noble character of bewailing the times and pitying the people and his incarnation as a hailstone god. Li Zuoju's Legends is rich in content, exaggerated plots and imagination. They cover people's understanding and evaluation of history and their resulting love and hatred for it. It has high literary and folk value. June 27 is the birthday of Li Zuoju, God of Hail. Every June, local people spontaneously organize activities to commemorate Li Zuoju, so as to promote his spirit of fighting evil, promoting goodness and benefiting the people.

Zou Xueshun has a profound knowledge of Chinese traditional culture. He has long been engaged in the collection, collation and research of Li Zuoju's Legends, enthusiastically disseminating folk culture. He has launched many initiatives and generously invested in the construction of the Li Zuoju Memorial Hall. His long-term study and research has laid a solid foundation for the development and inheritance of Li Zuoju's Legends.

Zou Xueshun mainly uses popular and easy-to-understand artistic techniques to tell Li Zuoju's Legends in the form of storytelling. The positive stories and thought-provoking teachings guide people to cultivate the spirit of creativity, the spirit of justice to praise virtue and punish vice, the spirit of humanity to bewail the times and pity the people, and the spirit of patriotism to advocate morality, which can play a role in strengthening moral accomplishment and enhancing humanistic accomplishment.

In 2012, Zou Xueshun won the exhibition award of successors of the 2nd China Intangible Cultural Heritage Expo. Over the years, he has made great efforts to explore, study and contribute Li Zuoju's Lengends. He has publicized Li Zuoju's Legends to the masses at the Li Zuoju Memorial Hall, collected pictures, manger, rooftop pillars and other materials about Li Zuoju's Legends, raised funds to build the bronze statue of Li Zuoju, and collected valuable materials for later generations to study Li Zuoju's Legends.

傳承人

传统音乐

Traditional Music

山东古筝乐传承人——祝妍芳

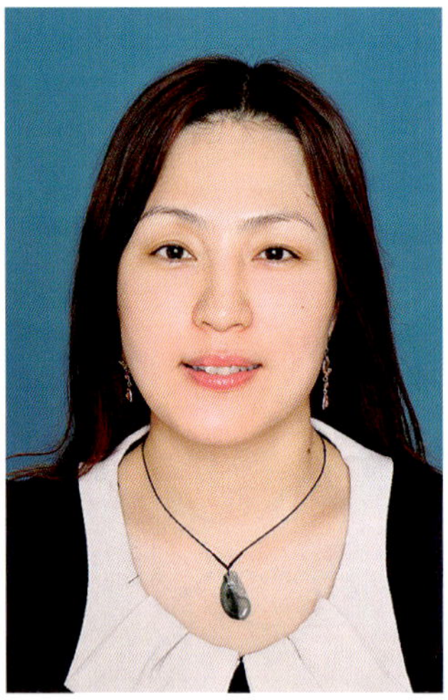

祝妍芳，女，1975年出生，山东菏泽人。

山东菏泽的古筝艺术有着悠久的历史传统，最早的文献记载可以追溯到汉魏时期，诗人曹植任鄄城王时，根据当时鄄城一带古筝艺术盛行的景象，写下了“弹筝奋逸响，新声妙如神”的诗句。菏泽古筝乐代表人物有王殿玉、赵玉斋、张应易等，其传统曲目和富有特色的演奏技法，是我国古筝艺术的瑰宝。

祝妍芳自学艺以来，一直刻苦钻研，勤奋好学。1982年，师从山东艺术学院教授韩廷贵学习古筝；1990年，考入菏泽市艺术学校专攻古筝独奏及伴奏；1993年，担任曲阜六艺城古筝独奏演员及乐队队长；1994年，分配到菏泽市群众艺术馆培训部工作至今；1995年创办妍芳古筝学校，教授古筝专业。

祝妍芳自幼就对古筝乐有深厚的感情，既对民间流传的牌子曲有一定的继承发展，还教好地掌握了现在流行的名曲，而且在合奏中还会结合姊妹艺术，取长补短。她学艺之余，勤于思考，于2012年6月在国家级刊物《戏剧丛刊》上发表论文《古筝赋》。

祝妍芳自1982年师从韩廷贵老师学习古筝，还曾得到古筝大师曹正先生、王世璜先生、赵登山先生的亲自指导，后又师从古筝演奏家李萌老师、赵曼琴老师、王中山老师、赵林老师学习。在创办古筝学校期间，她先后培养了1000多名古筝学员，为传承古筝艺术、推进山东古筝乐的发展起到了重要作用。

祝妍芳多次参加全国、省、市文艺会演，并获得了很多荣誉、奖项。如：1996~2008年，分别获中国音乐学院、中国民族管弦乐学会优秀指导老师奖；2002年12月，在菏泽市民族器乐大赛中，获专业组一等奖；2006年，获夏华杯中国民族器乐大赛优秀奖；2007年，其演奏的《包愣调》获山东省第一届艺术节金奖。

Zhu Yanfang—Inheritor of Shandong Guzheng Music

Zhu Yanfang, female, was born in Heze, Shandong Province in 1975.

The Guzheng art in Heze, Shandong Province, has a long historical tradition. The earliest documentary that recorded the Guzheng art can be dated to the Han and Wei Dynasties. When the poet Cao Zhi governed Juancheng City as the king, he visualized the prevailing scene of Guzheng Art in Juancheng area in his poem line "Playing the Guzheng forcefully and wonderfully, enjoying the heavenly fantastic music." The representative figures of Heze Guzheng music include Wang Dianyu, Zhao Yuzhai and Zhang Yingyi, etc. Its traditional music pieces and unique playing techniques greatly enrich the cultural treasury of Chinese Guzheng art.

Zhu Yanfang has been working hard and eager to learn since she began studying art. In 1982, she took Han Tinggui, a professor of Shandong University of Arts as her teacher in Guzheng. In 1990, she was admitted to Heze Art School of Shandong Province to specialize in Guzheng solo and accompaniment. In 1993 she became the Guzheng soloist and bandleader of the Confucius Six Arts City of Qufu. In 1994, she was assigned to the Training Department of Heze Museum of Mass Art, and has been working there ever since. In 1995, she founded Yanfang Guzheng Training School and also taught at the school.

Zhu Yanfang has been cherishing much affection for Guzheng music since her childhood. She not only inherits and develops the famous folk tunes (Paizi Qu in Chinese Pinyin), but also has a good grasp of the famous popular tunes. Besides, she combines Guzheng with other sister art forms in the performance to make them promote and complement each other. In the extracurricular time she ponders over what she has learned. In June, 2012, she published a paper "On Guzheng Art" in a key journal.

Besides being the apprentice to Professor Han Tinggui, she has received personal instruction from such great masters of Guzheng art as Mr. Cao Zheng, Mr. Wang Shihuang and Mr. Zhao Dengshan. Later she was apprenticed to the Guzheng players Li Meng, Zhao Manqin, Wang Zhongshan and Zhao Lin. Her Yanfang Guzheng Training School has cultivated more than 1,000 trainees successively, which played a certain role in inheriting the art of Guzheng and promoting the development of Shandong Guzheng music.

Zhu Yanfang has participated in many national, provincial and municipal art performances and won many honors and awards. In October 1994, she attended the National Day performance at Beijing National Forest Exhibition Hall. During 1996 and 2008, she was awarded the Excellent Instructor Awards by China Conservatory of Music and China Nationalities Orchestral Music Society. In December 2002, she won the first prize of the professional group in Heze National Instrumental Music Competition. In 2006, she won the Excellent Award of Xiahua Cup Chinese National Instrumental Music Competition. In 2007, her performance *Baoleng Tune* won the gold medal in the first Shandong Art Festival.

郯马五大调传承人——柏文泰

柏文泰，男，1941 年出生，山东郯城人。

因集中流行于鲁南地区临沂市郯城、马头一带而得名的郯马五大调，又称“郯马调”，也称“淮调”“五大调”。郯马五大调大多由一人演唱，伴奏以三弦为主，其他乐器如二胡、柳琴、笛子、琵琶、竹板等可有可无，可增可减，有时还用瓷碟、瓷碗、瓷酒盅、竹筷等物品伴奏，不仅音响清脆动听，而且姿势优美，形式活泼，别具一格。

柏文泰出身于马头镇柏花园村的艺术之家，其父柏士奇酷爱音乐，擅长演奏民间乐器二胡、三弦等，尤爱唱五大调中的“淮调”。柏文泰自幼受家庭熏陶，11 岁就能识简谱，13 岁便能演唱淮调中的《恨别离》《楚霸王自刎乌江》等曲目。20 世纪 50 年代，柏文泰开始广泛接触郯马五大调，跟老艺人学习【玲玲调】【满江红】【大寄生草】【大调】等曲牌曲目。他擅长二胡和三弦演奏，在整个乐队中主要担任伴奏，在三弦演奏方面主要师承胡庆友。

柏文泰轻板、迭板都能唱，对【淮调】【满江红】【玲玲调】【大寄生草】这四种曲调有较为深入的研究，且熟练掌握了板、眼、过板、腰板、行腔等。在演唱和伴奏方面，他善于精雕细琢，唱功婉转细腻。特别值得称赞的是，柏文泰在传统唱腔的整理方面，有着自己的独特方法，他所填词编写的新曲目，如《采莲湖里稻花香》《喜迎香港回归》等，也普遍受到老百姓的喜爱和好评。

柏文泰热爱五大调，擅长弹唱，专注创作，对五大调有一定研究。2003 年，他与临沂市戏曲研究室张铁民先生共同创作的《鹿乳奉亲传千秋》在“书圣节”文化节演出中获金奖，并于 2009 年赴中央电视台“民歌中国”栏目参加展演。

Bai Wentai—
Inheritor of Tan Ma Five Major Tunes

Bai Wentai, male, was born in Tancheng County, Shandong Province in 1941.

Tan Ma Five Major Tunes, also known as "Tan Ma Tunes" "Huai Tunes" or "The Five Major Tunes", got the name in that they are concentrated in Tancheng and Matou areas of Linyi City in south Shandong. Most of Tan Ma Five Major Tunes are sung by one person with sanxian as the main accompaniment. Other instruments such as erhu, liuqin, flute, pipa, bamboo clapper are optional and can be added or subtracted. Sometimes they are accompanied by porcelain dishes, porcelain bowls, porcelain wine cups and bamboo chopsticks. The tunes are clear and crisp in sound, and the gestures of the players are elegant. In addition, the lively form also adds to the wonderful atmosphere.

Bai Wentai was born in an artistic family of Baihuayuan Village, Matou Town. His father, Bai Shiqi, loved music, especially loved singing the Huai tune in The Five Major Tunes, and was good at playing folk instruments such as erhu and sanxian. Bai Wentai was educated by his family from an early age. He could read numbered musical notation at the age of 11. And at the age of 13, Bai Wentai could sing such songs as *Hate to Leave* and *The Lord of Chu Committed Suicide by the Wujiang River* of Huai tunes. In the 1950s, Bai Wentai began to make extensive contacts with Tan Ma Five Major Tunes, learning from the old artists such tunes as Lingling Tune, Manjianghong (in Chinese Pinyin), Grand Parasite Grass and Grand Tune, and etc. He is good at playing erhu and sanxian. He plays accompaniment in the whole orchestra and has inherited sanxian playing skills mainly from his teacher Hu Qingyou.

Bai Wentai can sing both light clapper and laminate clapper of the Huai tune. He has sophisticated understanding of such four tunes as the Huai tune, Manjiang Hong, Lingling Tune and Grand Parasite Grass, and has a good command of clapper, eye, cross clapper, waist clapper and phonating. In terms of singing and accompaniment, he excels in elaborating, tactful and delicate skills. It is particularly commendable that Bai Wentai has his own set of methods in the arrangement of traditional singing tunes. His newly composed tunes, such as *Rice Flowers in the Lotus Lake* and *Welcoming the Return of Hong Kong*, are widely appreciated and praised by the people.

Bai Wentai ardently loves the Five Major Tunes, is good at playing and singing it, and concentrates on its artistic creation. He has certain ability on the research and inheritance of Five Major Tunes. In 2003, he cooperated with Mr. Zhang Tiemin of Linyi Opera Research Office to create *A Story of Deer Milk on Filial Piety*, the performance of which won the gold medal in Linyi Book Culture Festival. Later in 2009, he played it in the CCTV *Folk Song China* column.

鲁西南鼓吹乐传承人——陈建彬

陈建彬，男，1967 年出生，山东省巨野县万丰镇陈集村人。

鲁西南鼓吹乐，又称“吹响器”“吹呜哇”，是一种以唢呐为主要演奏乐器的民间音乐形式。由于唢呐乐曲表现力丰富，喜庆时诙谐幽默，引人发笑，悲伤时如泣如诉，催人泪下，是烘托气氛的重要音乐形式，因此，在农村每逢婚丧嫁娶、节日庆典，都少不了唢呐艺人忙碌的身影。

陈建彬出身于鼓吹乐世家，世代以鼓吹乐为生，是典型的家族式传承。据族谱记载，17 世祖陈鸿吉是清乾隆年间鼓吹乐名手。陈家班是巨野南部鲁西南鼓吹乐的代表性班社。陈建彬从小耳濡目染，8 岁起随父陈新建学艺。经过父亲的悉心教导和个人的刻苦演练，他 12 岁就开始登台演出。

陈建彬基本功扎实，技艺全面，表演大方，以演奏传统独奏曲见长，擅长地方戏曲、民间小调等咔戏，代表作有《打枣》《开门》《笛绞》《大锯缸》《唱大戏》等。为使鲁西南鼓吹乐这一优秀的民间艺术继续散发魅力，陈建彬秉持家族传统，将其技艺传授给其子陈振振、其女陈晴。与此同时，陈建彬长年服务乡里，多次参加演出活动并获奖，为鲁西南鼓吹乐的传承做着不懈努力。

2008 年，他演奏的作品《画乡之春》在“谁不说俺家乡好”——山东地方文艺大赛中获金奖；2010 年，他受邀参加第 29 届世界音乐教育大会；2010 年，他受邀参加中央电视台《我们有一套》教师节特别节目；2010 年，他演奏的鼓吹乐、吹咔戏《大平调》在山东省第二届农村文化艺术节民间器乐声乐比赛中荣获一等奖；2013 年，作品《唱大戏》进入中国第十届艺术节“群星奖”决赛。

Chen Jianbin—
Inheritor of Trumpet Music of Southwest Shandong

Chen Jianbin, male, was born in Chenji Village, Wanfeng Town, Juye County, Shandong Province in 1967.

The Trumpet Music of Southwest Shandong, also known as "blow instrument" (Chuixiangqi in Chinese Pinyin) or "wind instrument of the folk music" (Chuiwuwa in Chinese Pinyin), is a form of folk music with suona as the main instrument. Because of rich expressiveness of the music, which is amusing and humorous in joyous atmosphere and pathetic and touching in sorrowful events, the suona music caters to all senses and emotions in various festivals and events. Therefore, suona artists are indispensible for weddings, funerals, and festival celebrations in the countryside.

Chen Jianbin was born in a family of trumpet musicians, with generations living on trumpet music. It is typical family inheritance. According to genealogy records, Chen Hongji, the 17th ancestor, was a famous trumpet musician during the Qianlong Reign of the Qing Dynasty. The Musical Society of the Chens (Chenjiaban in Chinese Pinyin) is representative of musical societies in the Trumpet Music of Southwest Shandong at the south of Juye County. Having been immersed in the atmosphere, Chen Jianbin started learning from his father Chen Xinjian at the age of 8. Under his father's careful instruction, and through his assiduous practice, Chen Jianbin performed on stage at the age of 12.

Chen Jianbin has solid basic skills, comprehensive techniques, and is natural and poised in his performance. He is good at traditional solos, kaxi (the name of a kind of ensemble in Chinese Pinyin) including local operas, folk minors, etc. His representative works include *Catch Jujube, Opening Door, Winding Flute, Big Saw Cylinder* and *Drama Show* (Changdaxi in Chinese Pinyin), etc. In order to develop and expand the charm of the excellent folk art of the Trumpet Music of Southwest Shandong, Chen Jianbin upholds the family tradition and imparts his skills to his son Chen Zhenzhen and his daughter Chen Qing. At the same time, Chen Jianbin has served the countryside for many years. He participated in performances and won awards many times, and made unremitting efforts for the inheritance of the Trumpet Music of Southwest Shandong.

In 2008, his work *Who Don't Praise My Hometown* won the gold medal in Shandong Local Literature and Art Television Competition. In 2010, he was invited to participate in the 29th World Conference on Music Education, and was also invited to participate in the special program of CCTV for Teachers' Day *We Have Our Own Way.* Also in 2010, his performance of the trumpet music and *Kaxi Daping Diao* won the first prize in the folk instrumental vocal music competition of the second Rural Culture and Art Festival of Shandong Province. In 2013, the work *Drama Show* entered the final of the stars award of the 10th Chinese Arts Festival.

古琴艺术传承人——庞雨珠

庞雨珠，男，1935 年出生，山东夏津人。

诸城派古琴是中国近代以来著名的古琴流派之一，具有兼收并蓄、勇于创新的艺术特点。诸城派古琴有独特的“以三弦为宫，以律吕命调”的立调体系以及粗犷、豪放、坚毅、醇厚、朴实、典雅、刚柔并济的演奏风格。它既继承了明清以来清微淡远的传统，又独具反传统、开创性、贴近民生、乡土气息浓郁、地域性的独特风格，在中国琴史上具有不可替代的地位。

庞雨珠师从诸城派第四代传人著名琴家张育瑾。因为悟性高，加之十分用功，他很快便掌握了古琴演奏技艺。1960 年 7 月，毕业于山东艺专音乐系后留校任教。1972 年 5 月，调德州市文化局工作。曾任中国古琴学会常务理事，山东琴会副会长；现为中国海洋大学、聊城大学艺术学院客座教授，聊城古琴学会特聘顾问。

庞雨珠古琴演奏水平高超，代表性曲目有《良宵引》《关山月》《长门怨》《平沙落雁》《流水》《梅花三弄》等，演奏风格坚毅、淳厚、古朴、典雅。

庞雨珠多年来从事古琴音乐艺术的理论研究，在各级各类报刊、杂志及理论刊物上发表论文 50 余篇，出版专著《古琴简明教程》《中国古琴音乐文集》等。其业绩记入《世界优秀专家人才名典》《中国当代创业英才》等多部专家名人集中。他曾多次参加各种古琴艺术活动，1985 年出席全国第三次古琴打谱会，1990 年出席中国古琴艺术国际交流会，1991 年出席首届国际孔子文化艺术节活动。庞雨珠一直在不同社会层次、不同文化程度的人群中举办各种类型的古琴培训班，以振兴和繁荣古琴音乐艺术，为古琴事业的传承做着不懈努力。

Pang Yuzhu—Inheritor of Guqin Art

Pang Yuzhu, male, was born in Xiajin County, Shandong Province in 1935.

Zhucheng School of guqin has been one of the famous schools of guqin since the 1840s. It has the artistic characteristics of being both inclusive and innovative. It has its unique vertical regulation system of "the main instrument sanxian interpreted by the musical temperament", and is characterized by its rough, bold, resolute, mellow, simple, elegant, rigid and soft performance style. It not only inherits the slight and distant tradition since the Ming and Qing Dynasties, but also develops a unique style of anti-tradition, pioneering, reflecting folk life, rich local flavor and unique regionalism, so it has an irreplaceable position in the history of Chinese qin.

Pang Yuzhu learned from Zhang Yujin, a famous pianist of the fourth generation of Zhucheng School. Because of his keen understanding and hard work, he soon mastered the skills of playing guqin. In July 1960, after graduating from the Music Department of the former college of Shandong University of Arts, he stayed in school to teach. In May 1972, he was transferred to Dezhou Cultural Bureau. He was the executive director of China guqin Society and vice president of Shandong Qin Society. He is now a visiting professor of school of Art of Ocean University of China and Liaocheng University and a special consultant of Liaocheng Guqin Society.

Pang Yuzhu's guqin performance is superb. His representative tunes are *Liangxiao Yin, Guanshan Moon, Changmen Hatred, Sandy Beach Geese, Running Water, Three Stanzas of Plum Blossoms* and so on. His playing style is firm, mellow, simple and elegant.

Pang Yuzhu has been engaged in the theoretical research of guqin music art for many years. He has published more than 50 papers in various newspapers, magazines and theoretical journals. Two of them have won the first prize and the excellent thesis prize of Shandong Province respectively. He also published two books *Concise Course of Guqin* and *Collection of Chinese Guqin Music*. His achievements have been recorded in such expert or celebrity collections as *World Outstanding Expert Talents Code* and *China Contemporary Entrepreneurial Talents*. He has participated in various guqin art activities on many occasions. He attended the third National Guqin Music Concert in 1985, the International Exchange Meeting of Chinese Guqin Art in 1990, and the first International Confucius Culture and Art Festival in 1991. Pang Yuzhu has been holding various types of guqin training courses among people of different social strata and educational levels in order to revitalize and prosper the art of guqin music, and has been making unremitting efforts for the teaching and inheritance of guqin.

古琴艺术传承人——朱子易

朱子易，男，1938 年出生，山东济南人，曾任山东省音乐家协会古琴专业委员会会长。

朱子易于 1956 年拜济南古琴名家詹澄秋先生为师，入室学习古琴三年，先后学习了《平沙落雁》等琴曲 20 余首。1959 年，他凭借古琴特长进入济南市歌舞团，从事民乐演奏，并于 1996 年开始全身心投入古琴艺术传授和研究中。2004 年，朱子易成立“泉韵琴社”，并任社长至今。2007 年，任山东艺术学院音乐学院客座教授，并在该院开设古琴专业，弘扬古琴艺术。

朱子易在继承詹澄秋清淡儒雅、刚中带柔特点的基础上，形成了古朴苍劲、挥洒自如的个人演奏风格。他在古琴艺术传授和研究过程中把相对和相近的指法组合在一起，用 14 句话概括了古琴常用的 56 种指法，并从中找出每一组指法的异同，方便了在对比中把握古琴的常用指法。除此之外，朱子易在总结前人经验的基础上，提出了一个吟猱处理新方法，定义了“小吟”“转吟”“大吟猱”“折猱”四个指法新概念，提高了古琴教学的系统性和规范性。

朱子易致力于古琴艺术的传承与发展，积极参加琴事活动，发表多篇论文，传授学生 200 余人。其学生大多从事相关专业的教学和研究工作。目前，一些学生已经开始成立琴社，传授自己的学生。

Zhu Ziyi—Inheritor of Guqin Art

Zhu Ziyi, male, born in Jinan, Shandong Province in 1938, was once the chairman of Guqin Professional Committee of Shandong Musicians Association.

In 1956, Zhu Ziyi took Mr. Zhan Chengqiu, a famous guqin master in Jinan, as his teacher. Through three years of his personal instruction, Zhu Ziyi learned more than 20 pieces of guqin music, such as *Sandy Beach Geese*, and etc. In 1959, he entered the Song and Dance Troupe of Jinan City with guqin as his specialty and engaged in folk music performance. In 1996, he began to devote himself wholeheartedly to the teaching and research of guqin art. In 2004, Zhu Ziyi founded the Quanyun Qin Society and has been the president since then. In 2007, he became a visiting professor of School of Music, Shandong University of Arts, and set up guqin major in this school to promote guqin art.

Zhu Ziyi inherited Zhan Chengqiu's light, elegant, rigid and gentle characteristics, and formed a simple, vigorous and free personal playing style. In the process of teaching and researching guqin art, he has combined different and similar fingerings, summarized 56 kinds of fingerings commonly used in guqin with 14 sentences, and found out the similarities and differences among groups of fingerings, which facilitates grasping the frequent fingerings of guqin in comparison. In addition, Zhu Ziyi has put forward a new method of guqin fingering named Yinnao, and defined four new fingering concepts namely "Xiaoyin" "Zhuanyin" "Dayinnao" and "Zhenao", which has improved the systematism and standardization of guqin teaching.

Zhu Ziyi has been devoting himself to the inheritance and development of guqin art. He has actively participated in guqin art activities, published many papers and supervised more than 200 students. Most of the students are engaged in the teaching and research work of related majors. At present, some students are setting up guqin clubs to teach their students.

傳承人

传统舞蹈

Traditional Dance

龙灯扛阁传承人——李玉常

李玉常，男，1953 年出生，山东临沂人。

龙灯扛阁是龙舞和扛阁结合在一起表演的广场舞蹈，发源于山东省临沂市，迄今已有 200 余年的历史。龙灯扛阁分为龙灯和扛阁两部分，两者有机结合为一个整体。龙灯表演由擎珠者指挥，龙体紧随龙珠舞动，套路均以“速场”贯穿连接。扛阁则以“走场”为主，龙舞动作激烈时，扛阁在一侧交叉变换队形；舞龙舒缓时，扛阁即插入龙队中穿行回旋。整个表演，龙体在翻滚卷起的雾霭中时隐时现，给人以驾云腾飞之感。龙灯扛阁粗犷奔放、气势恢宏，具有浓厚的北方民风习俗特征。

李玉常出生于“龙灯扛阁”世家，祖上几辈都是玩“龙灯扛阁”的。李玉常 2 岁上“扛”，15 岁参与舞龙，18 岁正式演出，25 岁学会扎制彩龙并担任教练工作。1970 年起，李玉常向“龙灯扛阁”表演代表性人物马守善、谷继春等老艺人学习舞龙技艺、扎糊彩龙，现为“龙灯扛阁”传承的主要艺人。

李玉常在掌握现有技艺的基础上有所创新发展，2000 年后发明扎制了“竹节龙”“荷花龙”“草龙”等，并将这些道具应用到龙灯表演中。在大龙舞动时，配上“荷花龙”和“草龙”等小巧灵活的道具，当中穿插扛阁，活灵活现，让人心潮澎湃，动感十足。

2000 年，李玉常参加首届“重庆·中国铜梁龙灯艺术节”，荣获“齐鲁神威奖”；2009 年，在济南参加全运会开幕式，荣获山东省政府、宣传部的奖项；2010 年，在上海世博会山东周开幕式和世博会巡游演出，取得圆满成功。李玉常还十分注重对于“龙灯扛阁”的传承与发扬，目前，已教授 13 名徒弟，培训舞龙表演者多达 300 人，为龙灯扛阁的传承发展做出了突出贡献。

Li Yuchang—Inheritor of Dragon and Pavilion Dance

Li Yuchang, male, was born in Linyi, Shandong in 1953.

Dragon and pavilion dance is a square dance comprising dragon dance and pavilion show. It originated in Linyi City, Shandong Province, and has a history of more than 200 years. It comprises two parts: dragon dances and pavilion shows, which are organically integrated into a whole. The dragon dance performance is directed by the bead bearer, and the dragon body dances closely with the bead. All the routines are connected by a "velocity field" (suchang in Chinese Pinyin). The pavilion show is dominated by a "walking field" (zouchang in Chinese Pinyin). When the dragon dance is intense, the pavilion show changes its formation on one side. And when the dragon dance is relaxed, the pavilion show is inserted into the dragon team to go through the circle. Throughout the whole performance, the dragon body appears and disappears in the rolling mist, giving people a sense of flying in the clouds. Dragon and pavilion dance is bold, unrestrained and magnificent, with strong characteristics of northern folk customs.

Li Yuchang was born in a family of dragon and pavilion dance, with his ancestors playing it for generations. At the age of 2, Li Yuchang performed in pavilion shows. He took part in dragon dance at the age of 15, and performed formally when he was 18 years old. At the age of 25, he learned to tie colored dragons and worked as a coach. Since 1970, Li Yuchang has begun learning dragon dancing skills and dragon making methods from the old artists such as Ma Shoushan and Gu Jichun, who are the representative performers of dragon and pavilion dance. He is now the main inheritor of the art of dragon and pavilion dance.

Li Yuchang has made innovations and progress on the basis of mastering the existing skills. After 2000, he invented and tied "Bamboo Dragon" "Lotus Dragon" "Grass Dragon" and so on, and applied these props to the dragon lantern performance. When the dragon dances, it is equipped with small and flexible props such as "Lotus Dragon" and "Grass Dragon", among which the pavilion is interspersed. The vivid and lively scene makes the audience excited and energetic.

In 2000, Li Yuchang participated in the first Chinese Tongliang Dragon Lantern Art Festival in Chongqing and won the Qilu Shenwei Award. In 2009, he participated in the opening ceremony of the National Games in Jinan and won the prizes awarded by the government. In 2010, he performed successfully at the Shandong Week Opening Ceremony of the Shanghai World Expo and the World Expo Tour. Li Yuchang also attaches great importance to the inheritance of dragon and pavilion dance. At present, Li Yuchang has taught 13 apprentices, given patient guidance to dragon dance enthusiasts, trained up to 300 dragon dancers, and made outstanding contributions to the inheritance of dragon and pavilion dance skills.

盐垛斗虎传承人——张良一

张良一，男，1955 年出生，山东东营人，现为东营斗虎艺术团团长。

盐垛斗虎，又名“打虎”，起源于东营市东营区龙居镇盐垛村，至今已有 100 多年的历史。盐垛斗虎借用老虎的抓、扑、咬、冲、跃、拍、剪等动作编排而成，动作粗犷、幅度大，有晃胯、扭腰、踢腿等高难度动作，表演中的转身、走步、跃虎等动作均有一定的技巧性。伴奏采用民间打击乐，表演者动作要合上鼓点的节奏。盐垛斗虎表演时先由教师爷用钓鱼鞭在锣鼓声中表演，打出一个直径约 50 米的圆场，名曰“开场子”。随后由 2 名武术水平较高的队员充当打虎英雄，4 人扮演老虎上场表演。两只老虎跑跳翻滚，摇头摆尾，千姿百态；2 名打虎英雄引逗老虎，在锣鼓声中做出各种武打和舞蹈动作，中间穿插高跷、旱船表演等，场面蔚为壮观。

张良一自幼跟随祖辈学习斗虎舞蹈，深得前辈真传。自 1979 年开始，张良一在务农期间，组建村内斗虎表演队，既是主演又是教练，参与斗虎舞蹈表演，活跃在乡村的舞台上。张良一现任东营斗虎艺术团团长，组队参加市、区春节和元宵节文艺会演，到各地进行斗虎串演，均得到很高的评价。

2003 年，张良一积极对盐垛村盐垛斗虎表演队进行重组，配合上级文化部门做好斗虎舞的普查工作，并协调镇、村两级投入资金进行改编创新，使这一古老的民间舞蹈艺术重新焕发生机。当前，以张良一为代表的传承人，担负起了盐垛斗虎的传承任务。张良一曾聘请省内相关专家对舞蹈进行排练，通过拍摄录像片、采访、收集录音资料等形式对斗虎舞进行记录与保存，对盐垛斗虎舞的传承与发展起到了积极的作用。

Zhang Liangyi—Inheritor of Yanduo Tiger Fighting

Zhang Liangyi, male, born in Dongying, Shandong Province in 1955, is now the head of Dongying Tiger Fighting Art Troupe.

Yanduo Tiger Fighting, also known as Striking Tiger, originated in Yanduo Village, Longju Town, Dongying District, Dongying City, and has a history of more than 100 years. It refers to such tiger movements as grasping, pouncing, biting, rushing, jumping, patting and scissoring, and etc. It is rough and wide, and has difficult movements such as shaking hip, twisting waist and kicking legs. The turning, walking and jumping in the performance all require certain skills. The accompaniment is folk percussion music, and the performer's movements should cater to the rhythm of drums. In the performance of Yanduo Tiger Fighting, a great master first performed in the sound of gongs and drums with a fishing whip, creating a circle about 50 meters in diameter, which is called the opening (kaichangzi in Chinese Pinyin). Then two players with high martial arts level act as heroes fighting tigers, and four people act as tigers. Two tigers run, jump, roll, shake their heads and tails, and pose in all kinds of ways. Two tiger fighting heroes tease tigers and make all kinds of martial arts and dancing movements in the sound of gongs and drums. With stilts and dry boat performances at intervals, the scene is spectacular.

Zhang Liangyi learned tiger fighting dance from his ancestors when he was young. He was deeply appreciated and acquired the essence. In 1979, when he was still a farmer, Zhang Liangyi organized a village tiger fighting performance team, for which he was both a leading actor and a coach. He participated in the tiger fighting dance performances and was active on the rural stages. Zhang Liangyi is currently the head of Dongying Tiger Fighting Art Troupe. His team has received high praise for participating in the performances of literature and art of the Spring Festival and Lantern Festival in cities and districts and performing a series of tiger fights in various places.

In 2003, Zhang Liangyi actively restructured the Yanduo Tiger Fighting Performance Team in Yanduo Village, cooperated with the superior cultural departments to do a good job in the survey of the tiger dance, coordinated the investment of funds at the town and village levels for the adaptation and innovation, and revitalized the ancient folk dance art. At present, Zhang Liangyi, as the representative of the inheritors, has taken on the task of inheriting Yanduo tiger fighting. Zhang Liangyi invited relevant experts from Shandong Province to rehearse the dance. He tried to record and preserve the dance through videos, interviews and collecting recording materials, which played a positive role in the inheritance and development of the dance.

孙斗跑驴传承人——孙奎山

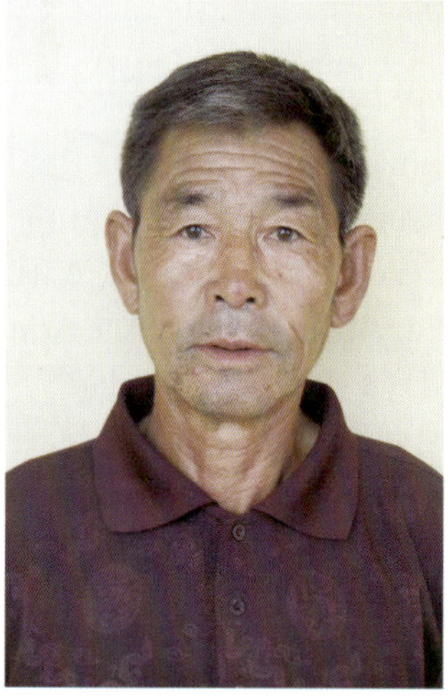

孙奎山，男，1946年出生，山东省东营市广饶县陈官乡人。

跑驴，又称“小黑驴”“ 小毛驴”，是流传于德州市和东营市广饶县的一种传统舞蹈形式。跑驴大多为双人表演，一人扮骑驴妇女，把驴形道具系在腰间，上身做骑驴状，以腰为中心，左右小晃身，下身用颤抖的小步蹭动，模拟驴的跑、颠、跳、踢、惊、犟等动作和神态。跑驴一般都是表现一对农村新婚夫妻在回娘家的路上过沟、爬坡、驴惊、抢救等经过，有说有舞，诙谐风趣。跑驴是鲁北地区较为典型的民间舞蹈文化之一，既体现了当地的文化特色，也反映了文化交融的历史脉搏。

跑驴的主要伴奏乐器有高音鼓、高音锣、钹镲、手锣等，烘托表演的气氛和节奏。跑驴的表演形式由原来的一骑一赶的单驴发展到现在的对驴和驴队，即由多对驴组成，一骑一赶为一组。以“别篱笆”“串花”变换队形，交换位置；在规定范围内大家做勒嚼、着鞭、踢腿、尥蹶等动作；锣鼓、串铃、响鞭等声响构成了跑驴舞蹈独特的交响乐。孙斗跑驴表演风格热闹、幽默、滑稽，故事情节丰富、质朴，表演形式多样。

孙奎山自幼跟随孙斗跑驴传人孙开山学习跑驴，掌握了跑驴的各种技巧。从1961年至今，孙奎山在务农期间积极参加民间文化节和艺术表演，获得许多奖项。2005年，孙奎山被东营市文化体育局授予“东营市文化能人”荣誉称号；2012年，荣获广饶县庆元宵特色民间艺术表演优秀表演奖；2013年，荣获陈官乡第五届民间艺术展演特等奖。与此同时，孙奎山充分利用农闲时间，组织跑驴成员进行培训与排练，提高孙斗跑驴成员的基本功；还将孙斗跑驴引进校园，在陈官乡初中成立了培训基地，开展孙斗跑驴的普及性教育，为孙斗跑驴的传承发展做出了贡献。

Sun Kuishan—Inheritor of Sundou Riding Donkey Dance

Sun Kuishan, male, born in 1946, is a native of Chenguan township, Guangrao County, Shandong Province.

Riding Donkey, also known as Little Black Donkey or Little Donkey, is a traditional dance form which is popular in Dezhou City and Guangrao County of Dongying City. Riding Donkey Dances are mostly performed in pairs. One person acts as a donkey-riding woman. She fastens donkey-shaped prop around her waist and makes donkey-like riding with her upper body. With her waist as the center, she sways around slightly. Her lower body runs with trembling small steps to simulate donkey's running, bumping, jumping, kicking, startling and stunning. Riding donkey generally shows a rural couple newly married on their way to the home of the wife's parents. With actors talking and dancing in the scenes of passing ditches, climbing hills, donkey shock, rescue and so on, the performance is witty and funny. Riding donkey is one form of the typical folk dance culture in north Shandong. It not only embodies the local cultural characteristics, but also reflects the historical pulse of cultural blending.

The main accompaniment instruments for Riding Donkey Dances are treble drums, treble gongs, cymbals and hand gongs, which set off the atmosphere and rhythm of the performance. The performance form of riding donkey has developed from a single donkey with one person riding and one person chasing to a pair of donkeys and donkey teams. A donkey team consists of many pairs, with each pair riding and chasing a donkey. The formation and position changes in the form of "fence dancing" and "flower string". Within the prescribed scope, performers do such actions as choking, whipping, kicking and kicking back. The sounds of gongs and drums, bells and whips

constitute the unique symphony of Riding Donkey Dance. Sundou Riding Donkey Dance is lively, humorous and funny. The story is rich and plain, and the performance forms are diverse.

In his childhood, Sun Kuishan learned Riding Donkey from Sun Kaishan, an inheritor of Sundou Riding Donkey Dance, and mastered various skills. Since 1961, Sun Kuishan has actively participated in folk culture festivals and artistic performances as a farmer career and won many awards. In 2005, Sun Kuishan was awarded the honorary title of Dongying Cultural Talent by Dongying Cultural and Sports Bureau. In 2012, he was awarded the Excellent Performance Award in Guangrao County Lantern Festival Characteristic Folk Art Performance. In 2013, he was awarded the special award in the Fifth Folk Art Exhibition Performance of Chenguan Township. Meanwhile, Sun Kuishan made full use of his leisure time to organize training and rehearsal of donkey riding members, so as to improve their basic skills. He also introduced Sundou Riding Donkey Dance into the campus, established a training base in Chenguan Township Junior Middle School, and carried out the popularization education of the dance, which contributed to the inheritance of Sundou Riding Donkey Dance.

戏灯穿花传承人——马洪贵

马洪贵，男，1952 年出生，山东栖霞人。

戏灯穿花，又名“穿花舞”，产生于元朝，发展于明清，流传于栖霞市臧家庄镇一带。“戏灯”由花盆、纸花和蜡烛组成，演员男女各 12 人；“头灯”中 1 人是“戏灯穿花”的核心，另有不同角色的男女“灯花”各 10 余人。戏灯穿花是集音乐、戏曲、舞蹈、民歌等为一体的综合表演艺术，歌唱部分为十二月对花，又称“灯歌”，配乐以竹笛、笙、二胡、木鱼为主，队形变化主要有“剪子股”“八字”“四门斗”“龙摆尾”“双菱花”“蛇蜕皮”等。舞蹈时，由锣鼓打点指挥舞蹈的快慢和节奏的急缓，演员情绪热烈奔放，节奏形式多变，明快紧凑；花盆随舞蹈者起起伏伏，进进出出。不同的角色有不同的扮相，舞者的动作、表情也各不相同。

马洪贵自幼喜欢穿花表演，十几岁就跟随父亲马树好学习戏灯穿花。1966 年，马洪贵在务农期间积极组织并表演戏灯穿花。2012 年，在首届胶东民俗文化山会上，马洪贵排演的戏灯穿花连演三天，得到很高的评价。“戏灯穿花”的步法要求步子小而轻，花盆在胸前保持稳平，花儿颤动，烛而不灭。马洪贵是“戏灯穿花”的高手，他的表演热情洋溢、稳健有力，其凭借扎实的功底成为戏灯穿花的传承人之一。

1988 年，马洪贵参加县秧歌大赛，获得演出一等奖；2008 年，参加山东省“苹果之都杯”非物质文化遗产展演活动；2013 年，参加栖霞市果农才艺展演，荣获一等奖。马洪贵现任村穿花舞队的主要负责人，负责臧家庄镇泊子村穿花舞队的组织和教习工作，安排舞队成员排练和演出，指导戏灯穿花技巧练习，为戏灯穿花的传承贡献着力量。

Ma Honggui— Inheritor of Opera Lantern Flower Dance

Ma Honggui, male, was born in 1952 in Qixia, Shandong Province.

Opera Lantern Flower Dance (Xideng Chuanhua in Chinese Pinyin), also known as Flower Dance, originated in the Yuan Dynasty, developed in the Ming and Qing Dynasties, and has spread to Zangjiazhuang Town, Qixia City. “Opera lantern” consists of flower pots, paper flowers and candles. There are 12 actors and 12 actresses, with one headlamp as the core of Opera Lantern Flower Dance, and more than ten men and women acting different “lantern flowers”. Opera Lantern Flower Dance is a comprehensive performing art that integrates music, opera, dance, folk songs and so on. The singing part is December flower pairing, also known as “lamp song”. The supporting music is mainly composed of bamboo flute, sheng, erhu and wooden fish. The formation changes mainly include “scissors” “character of eight” “four doors fighting” “dragon swinging tail” “Shuangling flower”, and “snake molting skin”. In the dance, the gongs and drums beat the spot, directing the dance speed and pace, the emotions are warm and unrestrained, the rhythm form is changeable, bright and compact, and flower pots fluctuate with the dancers in and out. The different roles have different appearances and the dancers’ movements and expressions also differ.

Ma Honggui has been fond of flower dance since his childhood. In his teens he followed his father Ma Shuhao to learn Opera Lantern Flower Dance. In 1966, as a farmer, Ma Honggui actively organized and performed Opera Lantern Flower Dance. In 2012, at the first Jiaodong Folklore and Culture Mountain Conference, the performance by Ma Honggui was showed on three days successively and were highly praised. Opera Lantern Flower Dance requires small and light steps. On the basis of keeping the flower pot flat in front of the chest, the flowers quiver but the candles never go out. Ma Honggui is a master of Opera Lantern Flower Dance. His performance is enthusiastic, steady and powerful. With his solid performance foundation, Ma Honggui has become an inheritor of Opera Lantern Flower Dance.

In 1988, Ma Honggui participated in the Yangko Contest of Qixia County and won the first prize for performance. In 2008, he participated in the Intangible Cultural Heritage exhibition in Shandong Province. And in 2013, he participated in the Fruit Farming Talent Exhibition in Qixia City and won the first prize. Ma Honggui is currently the main person in charge of the village flower dance team. He is responsible for the organization and teaching of the flower dance team in Pozi Village, Zangjiazhuang Town. He arranges rehearsals and performances for the members of the dance team, directs the practice of the skill of Opera Lantern Flower Dance, and makes contributions to its inheritance.

傳承人

传统戏剧

Traditional Drama

柳腔传承人——袁玲

袁玲，女，1962年出生，山东即墨人，国家二级演员。

即墨柳腔始于清朝乾隆年间，在山东“本肘鼓”基础上发展演变而来。柳腔初期的演唱形式非常简单，伴奏仅用一只手锣、一只手鼓和一只竹板，后来受“四弦小调”的影响，采用“四弦胡琴儿”伴奏。初用弦乐时，拉与唱不相协调，艺人们就互相配合着往上“溜”，故被戏称为“溜腔”，后来艺人觉得不雅，便借用同音字定名为“柳腔”，这就是柳腔的由来。

1976年，袁玲进入即墨柳腔剧团工作。先后跟随刘永华、毛秀美、张秀云等柳腔老艺人学习柳腔。1989年，袁玲拜著名评剧表演艺术家新凤霞为师学习表演，艺术水平达到新的高度。

袁玲工花旦、青衣，擅演花旦。她的扮相俊秀端庄，嗓音委婉明亮，唱腔甜美悦耳，表演功底娴熟，唱、念、做、打俱佳。袁玲在行腔、念白方面吸收其他剧种精华，改变柳腔的“顿”“拙”，并针对不同剧情把复杂的旦角贴片，改为秀美的越剧扮相，在服装上也做了改进。袁玲善于刻画人物性格，并逐步用戏剧表演理论指导自己的舞台表演实践，将评剧表演艺术融入柳腔当中，表现角色丰富的内心世界，塑造出丰满生动的人物形象。

1982年，袁玲获山东戏剧演出月表演奖；1985年，获青岛市青年演员基本功比赛一等奖；1991年，获山东省地方戏中青年演员比赛三等奖；1992年，获全国“天下第一团”优秀剧目展演表演奖。袁玲长期从事柳腔的普及推广工作，多次参加戏剧比赛和演出；担任剧团辅导老师，亲授表演艺术和唱腔唱法，培养了一批柳腔青年演员；在老年大学开办柳腔辅导课，在全市中小学推广柳腔，为柳腔的传承和发展做出了突出贡献。

Yuan Ling—Inheritor of Liuqiang

Yuan Ling, female, born in Jimo, Shandong in 1962, is a second-class national actress.

Jimo Liuqiang originated in the Qianlong Reign of the Qing Dynasty and evolved from Shandong's "Benelbow Drum". Liuqiang's initial singing form was very simple. It was accompanied by a gong, a drum and a bamboo clapper. Afterwards, influenced by "sixian litte tune" "sixian huqin", it was accompanied by "sixian little tune". At the beginning of xian accompaniment, the pulling and singing were not in harmony, so the artists cooperated with each other to "slip" (liu in Chinese Pinyin) upwards. As a result, the performance was jokingly called "slip tune" (liuqiang in Chinese Pinyin). Later, since the artists felt the name indecent, they borrowed the homophone to name it "liu tune" (also liuqiang in Chinese Pinyin), which is the origin of Liuqiang.

In 1976, Yuan Ling joined Jimo Liuqiang Opera Troupe. She followed the old artists Liu Yonghua, Mao Xiumei and Zhang Xiuyun respectively to learn Liuqiang. In 1989, Yuan Ling took Xin Fengxia, a famous opera critic and performer as her teacher, to learn the performance, and reached a new height in her artistic level.

Yuan Ling focuses on Huadan and Qingyi, of which she is good at the former. Her appearance is handsome and dignified, her voice is euphemistic and bright, and her singing is sweet and melodious, her performing skills are exquisite. She excels in singing, reading, doing and playing. Yuan Ling absorbed the essence of the similar dramas in her phonating and speech, changed the "pause" and "clumsiness" of Liuqiang, and changed the complex Dan character patches to the beautiful costumes of the Shaoxing opera according to different plots, and made improvements in the costumes. Yuan Ling is good at portraying characters' personality, and gradually guides her stage performance practice with theatrical performance theory. She integrates the art of theatrical performance into Liuqiang, expresses her rich inner world and shapes full and vivid character images.

In 1982, Yuan Ling won the Performance Award of Shandong Drama Performance Month. In 1985, she won the first prize of Qingdao Young Actors Basic Skills Competition. In 1991, she won the third prize in Shandong Local Drama Young Actors Competition. In 1992, she won the performing award in the National "First Troupe" Excellent Drama Performance. Yuan Ling has been engaged in the popularization and promotion of Liuqiang Opera for a long time, and has participated in many drama competitions and performances. She has taught in drama troupes a new group of young Liuqiang performers by personally teaching them performing arts and singing methods. She has opened Liuqiang Course in the University for the Elderly, and has promoted Liuqiang in primary and secondary schools in the whole city. She has made outstanding contributions to the inheritance and development of Liuqiang.

山东梆子传承人——祝凤臣

祝凤臣，女，1968年出生，山东菏泽人，国家一级演员。

山东梆子是山东省主要地方剧种之一，主要流行于山东省西南部，至今已有300多年的历史。山东梆子表演动作粗犷、架式夸张，唱腔结构体制属板式变化体，主要板式包括【慢板】【二八板】【流水板】【非板】等，唱腔慷慨激昂、刚劲挺拔，主奏乐器为板胡，行当则以红脸、黑脸为主，传统剧目十分丰富，具有很高的历史文化价值。

祝凤臣12岁学艺，最初师从前辈“绿牡丹”毕德玉，1980年考入郓城县戏曲学校学习戏曲表演。1981年，祝凤臣进入山东梆子剧团，担任主要演员。1999年，祝凤臣任山东梆子剧团副团长。2008年，祝凤臣拜山东梆子国家级代表性传承人刘桂松为师，认真学习“刘派”唱腔艺术和表演技巧，艺术水平得到进一步提高。

祝凤臣生旦俱工，主攻青衣、花旦、刀马旦。祝凤臣基本功扎实，戏路宽广。其扮相俊美，嗓音纯正，音域宽厚，她的唱腔以明朗高亢、抑扬多姿为特色，表演细腻朴实，唱念做打兼备。祝凤臣根据自身嗓音特点改进演唱技巧，着重感情的融入，讲究以声传情，形成自己独特的艺术风格。

祝凤臣精心培育后备人才，倾力传授表演技巧和演唱技能，先后培养学生20余人。祝凤臣积极参与各类文化演出活动，吸引更多的人关注山东梆子的发展，为山东梆子的传承与发展做出了积极贡献。2001年，由祝凤臣担任主要角色的大型现代戏《选村官》获山东省“五个一精品工程奖”，她个人荣获表演二等奖；2007年，获第三届中国戏曲红梅大赛山东赛区表演一等奖；2009年，在山东省山东梆子中青年演员大赛中获得一等奖；2010年，荣获“山东省山东梆子十大名演”称号；2011年，其主演的《大唐巾帼》获山东省第四届“泰山文艺奖”。

Zhu Fengchen—Inheritor of Shandong Bangzi

Zhu Fengchen, female, was born in 1968 Heze, Shandong Province, a national first-class actress.

Shandong Bangzi is one of the main local operas in Shandong Province. It is popular mainly in southwest Shandong. It has a history of more than 300 years. Its performance is rough and exaggerated. The structure of the aria belongs to the plate-type changing structure. Its main plate-type includes "Adagio" "Erba Clapper" "Stream Clapper" "Fei Clapper", and etc. The aria is emotional and vigorous. The main musical instrument is banhu. The main characters are red-faced and black-faced. With comprehensive traditional repertory, it has significant historical and cultural values.

Zhu Fengchen began learning the art at the age of 12. She was first taught by her predecessor Bi Deyu whose nickname was "green peony". She was admitted to Yuncheng Opera School in 1980 and studied opera performance there. In 1981, Zhu Fengchen joined Shandong Bangzi Opera Troupe as a leading actress. In 1999, Zhu Fengchen was appointed Deputy Head of Shandong Bangzi Opera Troupe. In 2008, Zhu Fengchen took Liu Guisong, the national representative inheritor of Shandong Bangzi, as her teacher, and earnestly studied the singing and performing skills of "Liu Faction", thus further improving her artistic level.

Zhu Fengchen studied both Sheng and Dan, and she mainly focused on Qingyi, Huadan and Daomadan. Zhu Fengchen's basic skills are solid and her opera road is broad. She has beautiful appearance, pure voice and broad range. Her aria is characterized by being clear, high-pitched, rich and colorful. Her performance is delicate and simple, covering singing, reading, doing and playing. Zhu Fengchen improves her singing skills according to the characteristics of her own voice,

emphasizing emotional integration, highlighting voice conveying feelings, thus forming her own unique artistic style.

Zhu Fengchen carefully nurtured reserve talents, devoted herself to teaching performance and singing skills, and successively trained more than 20 disciples. Zhu Fengchen actively participated in various cultural performances, attracted more people to pay attention to the development of Shandong Bangzi, and made positive contributions to its inheritance and development. In 2001, the large-scale modern drama *Selecting Village Officials* starred by her won the Five Top Fine Work Award of Shandong Province, and herself won the second prize for the performance. In 2002, she won the sliver prize of Shandong Opera Golden Melody Competition. In 2003, she played Fan Lihua in the ancient costume drama *Laoyang Mountain*, and won the gold prize in the "National Flower Cup" Young and Middle-aged Actors Drama Performance Contest. In 2007, she won the first prize of Shandong Competition Area in the Third Chinese Drama Red Plum Contest. In 2009, she won the first prize in Shandong Bangzi Middle-aged and Young Actors Competition. In 2010, she won the title of Ten Famous Performers of Shandong Bangzi in Shandong Province.

莱芜梆子传承人——李长生

李长生，男，1963年出生，山东莱芜人，国家一级演员。

莱芜梆子又名“莱芜讴”，是发源于泰沂地区，流行于鲁中、鲁东广大地区的古老地方剧种，至今已有200多年的历史。莱芜梆子道白字正、声硬、音直，属板腔体剧种，主要板式包括【慢板】【流水板】【梆子戏】【散板】四大类别，其唱腔高亢雄壮、激越奔放，且以唱腔中的“讴腔”最有特色。莱芜梆子的表演也是极具特点，古装戏粗犷奔放、长于夸张，现代戏朴实生动、生活气息浓厚，地方特色浓郁，艺术风格独特。

1977年，李长生考入莱芜梆子剧团，拜著名莱芜梆子老艺人魏育升为师，得其亲传真授。李长生主攻小生和老生，表演工整大气，讲究人物。在唱法上，李长生保留了莱芜梆子的传统特色；在表演方面，李长生戏路宽，能塑造不同性格的人物，在莱芜梆子的舞台上独树一帜，成为知名演员。

李长生积极致力于莱芜梆子的传承、发展和创新。2000年，李长生任莱芜梆子剧团团长，负责莱芜梆子剧团的剧目建设。在他的策划下，剧团移植经典剧目，创排新剧目，重新梳理剧本、情节，在唱腔、舞美、服装、灯光的设计上保持剧种特色的同时糅入时代气息。另外，李长生肩负着培养后备力量的责任。在剧团排练期间，他示范并辅导排练，为培养莱芜梆子剧团的青年演员做出了贡献，起到了传、帮、带的模范作用。

2004年，李长生策划、指导的大型现代戏《钓鱼人》被中共山东省委宣传部授予山东省第七届精神文明建设“精品工程”入选作品奖，参加第八届山东文化艺术节获演出奖；2007年，导演小品《胖孬家丑》并饰演胖孬，获全省首届农民艺术节金奖；2009年，在《儿行千里》全省巡演中成绩突出，被记二等功一次；同年，获第九届山东文化艺术节新创作剧目奖；2010年，策划指导的戏曲小品《暖水袋痒痒挠》获全国第十五届群星奖。

Li Changsheng—Inheritor of Laiwu Bangzi

Li Changsheng, male, born in Laiwu, Shandong Province in 1963, is a national first-class actor.

Laiwu Bangzi, also known as "Laiwu Ou" (in Chinese Pinyin), originated in Taiyi area and is popular in the vast areas of central and east Shandong. It has a history of more than 200 years. Laiwu Bangzi is a kind of panel opera with distinctive characters, hard voice and straight tone. Its main types of panel opera include such four categories as "Adagio" "Stream Clapper" "Bangzi Opera" and "Scattered Clapper". Its aria is magnificent, vigorous and bold, with "ou" as the most distinctive part. Its performance is also extremely characteristic. The ancient costume opera is rough and unrestrained, and is good at exaggeration. The modern opera is simple and vivid, with strong flavor of life, strong local characteristics and unique artistic style.

In 1977, Li Changsheng was admitted to Laiwu Bangzi Opera Troupe. He took Wei Yusheng, a famous Laiwu Bangzi veteran artist as his teacher, and was taught by him in person. Li Changsheng specializes in Xiaosheng and Laosheng, and performs neatly and carefully. In singing, Li Changsheng retains the traditional characteristics of Laiwu Bangzi. In performance, Li Changsheng plays a wide range of characters with different personalities. Distinguished on the stage of Laiwu Bangzi, he become a well-known actor.

Li Changsheng is actively committed to the inheritance, development and innovation of Laiwu Bangzi. In 2000, Li Changsheng became the head of Laiwu Bangzi Opera Troupe and was responsible for the construction of the repertoire of the troupe. Under his plan, the troupe transplanted classical plays, created new ones, reorganized scripts and plots, and maintained the characteristics of operas in the design of singing, dancing, clothing and lighting while incorporating the atmosphere of the times. Moreover, Li Changsheng shouldered the responsibility of training reserve forces. During the rehearsal of the troupe, he gave model guidance. He contributed to the training of young actors of the Laiwu Bangzi Opera Troupe, and played a model role of transmission, assistance and guidance.

In 2004, the large-scale modern drama *Angler* planned and directed by Li Changsheng won the seventh "Excellent Project Award" of the Propaganda Department of the Shandong Provincial Committee and performance award of the eighth Shandong Cultural and Art Festival Performance Award. In 2007, the short sketch *Pangnao's Family Scandal* directed and starred by Li Changsheng won the gold prize of the First Peasant Art Festival of Shandong Province. In 2009, he made outstanding achievements in the provincial performance tour of *Children Travel Thousands of Miles*, and was conferred second-class merit by Laiwu Municipal Party Committee and Municipal Government. In the same year, he won the performance prize of the Ninth Shandong Cultural and Art Festival. In 2010, the Drama Sketch *Warm Water Bag Itching and Scratching* planned and directed by him was awarded the fifteenth National Stars Award.

TRADITIONAL DRAMA

大弦子戏传承人——李学珍

李学珍，男，1939年出生，山东菏泽人，国家三级演奏员。

大弦子戏是流行于鲁西南的一个古老剧种，迄今已有500多年的历史。大弦子戏是在元明俗曲小令的基础上，集民间俗曲之大成发展形成的多乐调的戏曲声腔类型，属于弦索声腔系统。大弦子戏曲牌繁多，韵味各异，结构严谨规范、曲调委婉，调式丰富多变、风格各异，其表演程式丰富，注重技巧技能，动作粗犷泼辣，架式夸张，武戏多用真刀真枪，文戏细腻典雅，地方特色鲜明，对研究元、明以来北方戏曲音乐、元散曲都有重要价值。

1956年，李学珍进入定陶县曙光大弦子戏剧团，拜大弦子戏主笛赵海如为师，学习记录曲牌唱腔；之后进入菏泽市地方戏曲传承研究院山东梆子剧团，研究大弦子戏，并在庞礼老师的指导和帮助下学习音乐、理论方面的知识，掌握了基本记谱要领，为挖掘、整理大弦子戏打下了基础。

1962~1963年，李学珍在濮阳大弦子戏剧团老艺人党福修、高连元的帮助下，挖掘整理了120多个古老曲牌，现保留曲牌300余支。1963年，李学珍为适应现代戏的人物塑造要求，大胆革新现代戏的音乐唱腔，对现代戏《江姐》《琼花》《雪岭苍松》等剧目的唱腔进行改革，使其更能清晰地表达现代人物的思想感情，演出后得到很高的评价，改革经验不断向其他兄弟剧团推广，使古老的弦子戏焕然一新。多年以来，李学珍先后挖掘整理大弦子戏古老曲牌150余支，传授曲牌唱腔80余支，并全部录音、录像，又翻制成谱，交给有关部门存档收藏，为后人学习研究大弦子戏留下了珍贵的档案和史料。

菏泽市大弦子戏保护工作启动以来，李学珍积极配合菏泽市地方戏曲传承研究院的工作，搜集、整理传统唱腔。退休后，他依旧致力于大弦子戏唱腔曲牌的挖掘、整理、谱曲、传承工作，积极参与大弦子戏的项目保护工作，为大弦子戏的传承与发展做出了贡献。

Li Xuezhen—Inheritor of Big String Opera

Li Xuezhen, male, born in Heze, Shandong Province in 1939, is a national third-class player.

Big String Opera is an ancient opera popular in southwest Shandong. It has a history of more than 500 years. Big String Opera is a multi-tone opera vocal tune type formed by the development of folk operas on the basis of folk tune "Xiaoling" in the Yuan and Ming Dynasties, which falls within the string vocal tune system. Big String Opera has a variety of brands, different charms, rigorous and standard structures, euphemistic tunes, rich and varied modes and different styles. With rich performance styles, it pays attention to techniques and skills. The movements are rough, unrestrained, and exaggerated. In the martial drama, it uses real knives and guns. And the literary operas are fine and elegant and distinctive with local characteristics. It is of great value to the study of northern opera music since the Yuan and Ming Dynasties and the study of Yuan Sanqu.

In 1956, Li Xuezhen entered the Shuguang Big String Opera Troupe in Dingtao County, where he took Zhao Hairu, the master flute of Big String Opera as his teacher and learned to record the tune of the opera clapper. Then he joined the Shandong Bangzi Opera Troupe of Heze Local Opera Inheritance Research Institute to study Big String Opera. With the guidance and help of Pang Li, he learned the knowledge of music and theory, grasped the essentials of the basic notation of Big String Opera, and laid the foundation of exploring and reorganizing Big String Opera.

From 1962 to 1963, with the help of Dang Fuxiu and Gao Lianyuan, the veteran artists of Puyang Daxianzi Drama Troupe, Li Xuezhen excavated and sorted out more than 120 ancient music brands, and now retained more than 300. In 1963, Li Xuezhen boldly innovated the musical tunes of modern operas in order to meet the requirements of the characterization of modern operas. He reformed the tunes of modern operas such as *Jiangjie, Qionghua* and *Xueling Cangsong*, so that they could express the thoughts and feelings of modern characters more clearly. After the performance, Li Xuezhen was highly appraised. His experience of reform was constantly extended to other brother troupes, and the ancient string operas were glorified. Over the years, Li Xuezhen has excavated and sorted out more than 150 old opera brands of Big String Opera, imparted more than 80 opera arias, recorded and made videos of them, turned them into music scores, and denoted them to the relevant departments to store away, which leaves precious archives and historical materials for future generations to learn and study Big String Opera.

Since the protection of Big String Opera in Heze started, Li Xuezhen has actively cooperated with the local opera inheritance research institute to collect and sort out traditional tunes. After retirement, he still devoted himself to the excavating, sorting out, composing and inheritance of Big String Opera tunes, and actively participated in the project protection of Big String Opera, contributing to the inheritance and development of Big String Opera.

四平调传承人——刘玉香

刘玉香，女，1964 年出生，山东金乡人。

四平调形成于 20 世纪 40 年代末，由流行于山东、江苏、河南、安徽四省接壤地带的一种民间说唱艺术“花鼓”发展演变而来，吸收评剧、京剧、梆子等剧种的曲调而成。四平调源于说唱艺术，以善唱著称，在四平调音乐中，唱腔音乐是它的主体，以板式变化体为主，以【平板】为主要曲调，运用戏曲音乐板式派生原则，派生出不同板式。四平调的唱腔和节奏的变化甚为自由灵活，旋律委婉缠绵，华丽多姿，可表达多种情感。四平调的传统剧目有《小借年》《陈三两爬堂》《三告李彦明》《小姑贤》《吕蒙正赶斋》等。

1976 年，刘玉香进入原金乡四平调剧团，跟随杜雪亭等老师学习四平调。1977 年，刘玉香登台演出，广受听众欢迎。1984 年，剧团整编，刘玉香被调至金乡县文化馆继续学习戏曲艺术。

刘玉香主攻青衣、老旦、小生，基本功扎实，嗓音高昂，清脆明亮，吐字清晰，唱腔圆润，扮相英俊，能栩栩如生地扮演多种角色。她深入分析人物性格特点，将不同个性的人物演得活灵活现，深受广大群众的喜爱。

2004 年，刘玉香参加河南省梨园春擂台赛获得 263 期擂主；2005 年，参加首届全国戏迷擂台赛获得优秀奖；同年，在金乡成功举办了刘玉香个人演唱会；2011 年，在济宁市票友大赛中获得一等奖;2012 年,在济宁市“迎十艺盛会　展济宁风采”地方戏曲票友大赛中获得金奖。刘玉香广收徒弟，培养业余戏曲爱好者近百人；2011 年，被聘为金乡县实验小学戏剧教师，进一步扩大了四平调的影响，为四平调的传承与发展做出了自己的贡献。

Liu Yuxiang—Inheritor of Siping Tune

Liu Yuxiang, female, was born in Jinxiang County, Shandong Province in 1964.

Siping Tune was formed in the late 1940s. It evolved from a folk rap art "flower drum" popular in the bordering areas of Shandong, Jiangsu, Henan and Anhui Provinces. It absorbed the tunes of Ping Opera, Peking Opera and Bangzi, and etc. Siping Tune originates from rap art and is famous for its good singing. In Siping Tune music, singing is dominant, with the change of "Flat Clapper" as its main melody, using the principle of derivation of the Flat Clapper type of opera music to derive different types of plate. The aria and rhythm change of Siping Tune is very free and flexible, and the melody is euphemistic and lingering, gorgeous and colorful, and capable of expressing a variety of emotions. The traditional operas in Siping Tune include *Xiaojienian* (in Chinese Pinyin), *Chen Sanliang Climbing Hall, Three Complaints on Li Yanming*, *Virtuous Aunt* and *Lü Meng Is Rushing for Temple Food,* and etc.

In 1976, Liu Yuxiang entered the then Jinxiang Siping Tune Opera Troupe and learned Siping Tune from Du Xueting and other teachers. In 1977, Liu Yuxiang appeared on the stage and was widely welcomed by the audience. In 1984, Liu Yuxiang was transferred to Jinxiang County Cultural Museum to continue studying opera art.

Liu Yuxiang specializes in Qingyi, Laodan and Xiaosheng. She has solid basic skills, crisp and bright high-pitched voice, clear pronunciation, mellow tunes, handsome appearance, and can play many roles vividly. She thoroughly analyzed the personality of each character, and presented different personalities vividly and lifelike, which greatly satisfied the masses.

In 2004, Liu Yuxiang participated in the Liyuanchun Challenge Match in Henan Province and won the 263rd series. In 2005, she took part in the first National Opera Fan Challenge Competition and won the excellent prize. In the same year, Liu Yuxiang successfully held his personal concert in Jinxiang County. In 2011, she won the first prize in Jining Fans Competition. In 2012, she won the golden prize in Jining Fans Competition of "Welcomeing Ten Arts Festival and Exhibiting Jining Charm". Liu Yuxiang received a wide range of apprentices and trained nearly 100 amateur opera enthusiasts. In 2011, she was hired as a drama teacher in Jinxiang Experimental Primary School, which further enhanced the influence of Siping Tune. She made considerable contribution to the inheritance and development of Siping Tune.

抻腔传承人——卞项颂

卞项颂，男，1956年出生，山东博兴人，国家一级演员。

抻腔发源于山东省博兴县，形成于17世纪中叶，清光绪年间达到鼎盛，是早期流行在山东境内的戏曲剧种之一，与五音戏、茂腔、柳琴戏颇有渊源。抻腔原名“肘鼓子”，演唱以真假嗓音混合唱，时粗时细，时高时低，强弱分明，既无弦乐伴奏，又常在板后起唱。抻腔的音乐为板腔体，由【慢板】【二板】【垛板】【散板】和曲牌组成。常用的唱腔曲牌有【枣娃娃】【柳娃娃】【莲花落】【辞弹】等。抻腔表演讲求唱、做、念、打、手、眼、身、法、步，行当分生、旦、净、丑，但所有行当的各种角色都由男演员担任。

卞项颂自幼喜欢戏曲，6岁学唱抻腔，师承张守勤。1970年，进入博兴县剧团，担任主要演员；1983年，担任博兴县剧团副团长、主要演员；1997年至今，担任博兴县剧团团长。

卞项颂从艺近40年，经过长期的舞台演出实践，根据自身的条件、性格特点和现代人的审美需求，对抻腔进行了有益的创造和发展，形成了粗犷豪放、细腻典雅的独特艺术风格。他的唱腔艺术内敛、含蓄、精美而富于韵味，将风格由媚婉向舒朗空灵、流畅华美拓展，讲求声腔的韵律感，把美感发展到了极致，是对抻腔艺术的延伸和创新。卞项颂塑造出众多栩栩如生的艺术形象，是抻腔表演艺术的代表人物之一。

卞项颂被评为“滨州市十佳戏剧人物”“山东省文化下乡先进个人”，其执导的抻腔剧《人间真情在》《好亲家》《笑笑为媒》分别获第二、三、九届小戏艺术节大奖。近年来，卞项颂积极投身于抻腔保护与传承工作，通过采风、采访抻腔发祥地的抻腔艺人等形式，搜集、整理剧目20余种，整理了大量的文献资料，掌握了抻腔的原生态资料，培养抻腔人才100余人，为抻腔的保护传承工作做出了突出贡献。

Bian Xiangsong—Inheritor of Den Qiang

Bian Xiangsong, male, born in 1956, is a national first-class actor from Boxing County, Shandong Province.

Den Qiang originated in Boxing County, Shandong Province, and was formed in the mid-17th century. It reached its peak in the Guangxu Reign of the Qing Dynasty. It was one of the early operas popular in Shandong Province. It had a lot to do with Wuyin Opera, Mao Qiang and Liuqin Opera. The original name of Den Qiang is "elbow drum". It is mixed with true and false voices. It is thick and thin, high and low, strong and weak. It has no string accompaniment and often goes after the rhythm. The music of Den Qiang is of a plate tune style, which is composed of "Slow Clappe" "Er Clapper" "Duo Clapper" "San Clapper" and qupai. The frequently used tunes include "Jujube Dolls" "Willow Dolls" "Lotus Falls" "Citan" and so on. Den Qiang performances emphasize singing, doing, reading, beating, hand, eye, body, mode and footwork. The types of roles cover Sheng, Dan, Jing and Chou, but all roles are exclusively played by male actors.

Bian Xiangsong has been fond of opera since his childhood. At the age of 6, Bian Xiangsong learned to sing Den Qiang and was taught by Zhang Shouqin. In 1970, Bian Xiangsong entered the Theatre Troupe of Boxing County as the main actor. In 1983, he became the deputy head and main actor of the Theatre Troupe of Boxing County. Since 1997, he has been the head of the Theatre Troupe of Boxing County.

Bian Xiangsong has been engaged in art for nearly 40 years. After a long period of stage performance practice, in accordance with his own conditions, personality characteristics and modern people's aesthetic needs, he has made innovations on and developed Den Qiang, and formed a unique straightforward and unrestrained, exquisite and elegant artistic style. His singing art is restrained, implicit, exquisite and full of charm. He develops his style from being melodious and graceful to being smooth and flowing. He emphasizes the rhythm of the voice and develops the aesthetic feeling to the extreme, which is the extension and innovation of the Den Qiang art. Bian Xiangsong has created many vivid artistic images, and he is one of the representatives of the performing arts of Den Qiang.

Bian Xiangsong was named "Ten Best Drama Persons in Binzhou City" and "Advanced Individuals to Send Culture to the Countryside in Shandong Province". The Den Operas *True Love on Earth*, *Good In-laws* and *Xiaoxiao as Matchmaker* directed by him won prizes in the second, third and ninth Small Opera Art Festivals of Shandong Province respectively. In recent years, Bian Xiangsong has actively devoted himself to the protection and inheritance of Den Qiang. Through collecting folk songs and interviewing Den Qiang artists, he collected and sorted out more than 20 plays, reorganized a large number of documents and materials, and grasped the original ecological information of Den Qiang. Bian Xiangsong has trained more than 100 talents of Den Qiang, and has made outstanding contributions to its protection and inheritance.

茂腔传承人——王淑娴

王淑娴，女，1943 年出生，山东胶南人，国家二级演员。

茂腔属山东省地方戏曲“肘鼓子”声腔系统，早期叫“本肘鼓”“轴棍子”“冒肘鼓”等，主要活跃于山东东部地区，距今已有 200 多年的历史。茂腔曲调质朴自然，唱腔委婉幽怨、通俗易懂，女腔尤为发达，给人以悲凉哀怨之感。茂腔初期只有鼓、钹、锣等打击乐伴奏，后来受京剧、梆子等的影响，采用京胡为主奏乐器，并用二胡、月琴配合，之后陆续增添唢呐、笛、笙、低胡、扬琴等民族乐器。茂腔的传统戏多为反映男女爱情、伦理道德等生活片段的小戏，颇受人民群众的喜爱。

1961 年，王淑娴考入胶南茂腔剧团，跟随马玉美老师学习茂腔，并开始登台表演；1964 年，进入高密茂腔剧团，担任主演；1966 年，担任胶南市茂腔剧团团长，兼任导演。从事茂腔艺术以来，王淑娴主演了 70 多出传统和现代剧目，塑造了众多艺术形象，得到广大观众的认可和好评，对发展地方文艺做出了突出贡献。

作为胶南茂腔的主要代表性人物，王淑娴善于改革创新，她设计的茂腔唱腔优美动听，感人至深。她扮相俊美，表演大方，吐字清晰，演唱纯真。她扮演花旦如行云流水，唱青衣稳重大方，唱老旦神情逼真。王淑娴的演技底蕴颇深，将众多人物形象演绎得活灵活现，她扮演的许多剧中角色已牢牢嵌印在人们的记忆里。

1981 年，王淑娴在新编神话剧《琅琊宝珠》中饰演大蛤，获青岛市会演一等奖；1997 年，在山东省青年演员观摩演出大会上获特殊贡献奖；1999 年，组织编排向国庆五十周年献礼的茂腔戏《生日》，获青岛市文化局剧目、导演、演员、唱腔等七个大奖；2002 年，在“中国戏曲名段演唱大赛”中获地方戏专业组二等奖。多年来，王淑娴经常带领茂腔剧团下乡镇演出，多次到基层茂腔艺术团进行传习，辅导和培训茂腔爱好者。王淑娴始终牵挂茂腔事业，为茂腔这一传统戏曲艺术的传承贡献力量。

Wang Shuxian—Inheritor of Mao Qiang

Wang Shuxian, female, born in Jiaonan, Shandong Province in 1943, is a national second-class actress.

Mao Qiang belongs to the "elbow drum" acoustic system of Shandong local opera. It was called "ben elbow drum" "axle stick" and "risen elbow drum" in its early stage. Mao Qiang was mainly active in east Shandong Province. It has a history of more than 200 years. Mao Qiang tune is simple and natural, euphemistic and plain, and easy to understand. The female tune is especially developed, giving people a sense of sadness and sorrow. In the early stage of Mao Qiang, it was only accompanied by such percussion music as drums, cymbals and gongs. Afterwards, influenced by Peking Opera and Bangzi, jinghu was used as the main musical instrument, and erhu and moon guitar were used to cooperate with each other. Later, suona, flute, Sheng, dihu and dulcimer were added one after another. Traditional Mao Qiang plays are mostly small plays reflecting love between men and women, ethics, and morality, and are very popular among the people.

In 1961, Wang Shuxian was admitted to Jiaonan Mao Qiang Troupe. She followed Ma Yumei to learn Mao Qiang and began performing on the stage. In 1964, she joined Gaomi Mao Qiang Troupe as the leading actor. In 1966, she was the head of Jiaonan Mao Qiang Troupe and also worked as the director. Since she was engaged in Mao Qiang art, Wang Shuxian has starred in more than 70 traditional and modern plays, created many artistic images, won the recognition and praise of the broad audience, and made outstanding contributions to the development of local literature and art.

As the main representative figure of Jiaonan Mao Qiang, Wang Shuxian is good at reform and innovation. Her Mao Qiang tune is beautiful and moving. She is handsome in appearance, generous in performance, clear in speech and pure in singing. She plays the role of Huadan skillfully, sings Qingyi in an elegant and steady manner, and sings the Laodan with a realistic expression. Wang Shuxian's acting skills are profound, and many characters are vividly presented. Many of the roles she plays are firmly have impressed the audience deeply.

In 1981, Wang Shuxian won the first prize of Qingdao Opera Performance for playing Big Clam in the newly-compiled mythological drama *Langya Jewelry*. In 1997, she won the special contribution prize at Shandong Youth Actors Demonstration Performance Conference. In 1999, her Mao Qiang Opera *Birthday*, which was organized and arranged for the 50th anniversary of the National Day, won seven big prizes, for the repertoire, director, actor, singing and so on. In 2002, in the Singing Competition of Famous Sections of Chinese Opera, she won the second prize in the professional group of local opera. Over the years, Wang Shuxian has often led Mao Qiang Opera Troupe to perform in villages and towns. She went to the grass-roots Mao Qiang Art Troupe many times for tutoring, coaching and training Mao Qiang enthusiasts. Wang Shuxian has always been concerned about Mao Qiang and contributed to the inheritance of Mao Qiang, a traditional opera art.

傳承人

山东省省级非物质文化遗产项目
代表性传承人

第四卷

曲艺
Folk Art Forms

曲艺

山东大鼓传承人——魏素英

魏素英，女，1949年出生，山东济南人。

山东大鼓，是我国北方最早的鼓曲形式，有着350余年的历史，原名“犁铧大鼓”，后因其“所唱皆山东土调”“唱者皆山东产”而通称“山东大鼓”。山东大鼓约产生于明中叶，明末清初开始独立门户，嘉庆年间发展出了五大分支，唱腔上形成了三大派别，清同光年间开始出现女演员，清末大兴，其间涌现出了许多山东大鼓班社和数十名著名艺人，像谢、李、孙、赵“四大玉”等人就是这一时期的名家。山东大鼓经过发展已成为成熟的曲艺形式，其音乐唱腔风格独特，男腔顿挫有力，女腔舒展优美，极具欣赏价值。

魏素英自幼爱好曲艺，11岁便拜“四大玉”中的谢大玉为师，系统地学习山东大鼓。谢大玉人称“十三红”，她说唱吐字清晰，嗓音高亢圆润，腔调婉转，表情传神，擅长金戈铁马的《单刀会》《古城会》《华容道》等曲目。她继承前辈之长，并吸收其他剧种之精华，丰富发展了山东大鼓的唱腔，是山东大鼓发展史上的重要人物。在跟随谢大玉老师多年学习中，魏素英刻苦努力，逐渐掌握了谢大玉老师的多种演唱方法和表演技巧。魏素英继承了谢大玉老师的表演风格，并多次跟随谢老师参加演出，丰富了自己的舞台实践，同时也提高了个人艺术水平。她嗓音高亢明亮，演唱委婉柔美，表演俊美大方，感情真切自然，舞台风格典雅优美，既能保持传统的风格，又独具特色。

1965年，魏素英参加济南市专业曲艺会演，演唱的山东大鼓《千里送暖》获演员表演一等奖。1974年，参加了全国曲艺调演工作。1975年，参加山东省曲艺会演，为山东大鼓《红嫂》装腔、排练，并参加了演出。如今，山东大鼓的盛况已不复当年，发展面临严峻挑战。魏素英作为传承人，积极培养下一代传承人，收徒授艺，其徒弟目前也小有名气，一代代的传承人正在为山东大鼓的发展努力着。

Wei Suying—Inheritor of Shandong Drum

Wei Suying, female, was born in Jinan, Shandong Province in 1949.

Shandong Drum is the earliest form of drum music in north China. It has a history of more than 350 years. Its original name was "plough drum". Later, it was commonly known as "Shandong drum" because it "sings all Shandong local tunes" and "all singers are Shandong natives". Shandong Drum came into being in the middle of the Ming Dynasty. In the late Ming Dynasty and the early Qing Dynasty it gradually became the independent school. During the Jiaqing Reign of the Qing Dynasty, five major branches were developed, and three major factions were formed as far as the singing tune was concerned. During the Tongzhi and Guangxu Reigns of the Qing Dynasty, the actresses began to appear. At the end of the Qing Dynasty, there emerged many Shandong Drum Group Societies and dozens of famous artists, such as the "Four Jades"— Xie, Li, Sun, Zhao. Through development, Shandong Drum has become a mature form of folk art. Its musical tune is unique. The male tune is frustrated and powerful, and the female tune is stretched and graceful. It is of great appreciation value.

Wei Suying has been fond of traditional Chinese opera since her childhood. At the age of 11, she took Xie Dayu, one of the "Four Jades", as her teacher and studied Shandong Drum systematically. Xie Dayu is known as "Thirteen Red". Her rap is clear, and her voice is loud, melodious and expressive. She is good at the heroic tunes, such as *Single Sword Appointment, Ancient City Meeting* and *Huarong Road*. She inherits the older generation and absorbs the essence of other dramas, enriching the tunes of Shandong Drum, and becomes an important figure in the history of Shandong drum development. During the many years of learning from Xie Dayu, Wei Suying worked hard and gradually mastered Xie Dayu's various singing methods and performing skills. Wei Suying inherited the performance style of Xie Dayu and performanced with her many times, enriching her stage practice and improving her personal artistic level. Her voice is high and bright, her singing is euphemistic and graceful, her performance is handsome and generous, her emotions are real and natural, and her stage style is elegant and graceful, all of which not only keep the traditional style, but also have their own characteristics.

In 1965, Wei Suying participated in Jinan professional musical performance. Her Shandong Drum *Thousands of Miles to Warm* won the first prize for performance. In 1974, she participated in the National Opera Performance. In 1975, she participated in the Shandong Quyi Festival, with *Red Sister-in-law*. Today, Shandong Drum is no longer as prosperous as before, and its development is facing serious challenges. Wei Suying, as an inheritor, actively trains the next generation of inheritors and receives apprentices, who are also well-known at present. Generations of inheritors are making effort for the development of Shandong Drum.

山东琴书传承人——魏务良

魏务良，男，1956年出生，山东济南人，济南市曲艺团国家一级演员。

山东琴书于清代初叶发源于鲁西南，早期为自娱自乐的民间演唱形式，有许多业余班社，形成了年节赛会的演唱习俗。音乐结构为联曲体形式，以《白蛇传》为主要演出曲目，连缀使用的曲牌多达300余支。清光绪末年，因灾荒，郓城的刘老继、金乡的李凤兴等玩友下海成为第一批职业艺人，逐渐变多人演唱为二三人操坠琴、扬琴等乐器自拉自唱的演出形式。音乐结构发展为以“老六门主曲”为主的主插体形式。

1978年，魏务良开始跟随著名南路山东琴书艺人李若亮、李湘云学习演唱南路琴书曲目《水漫金山》《寇准罢宴》《掐伙计》《鹧鸪天》等。1981年，魏务良正式拜李湘云为师，学习南路琴书的演唱方法和表演技巧。

魏务良在学习山东琴书的过程中，分析了山东琴书的演唱风格、韵味、吐字发声、板眼、设景、表演等特点。他把南路琴书和北路琴书的精华部分有机地结合在一起，南北串通，取长补短，优势互补，既唱出古曲的神韵，又增添了时代性。

魏务良设计的唱腔和编导的山东琴书节目已在全国、全省多次获奖。1986年，表演的山东琴书《亲上亲》在全国新曲书目会演中获文化部铜奖。1989年，表演的山东琴书《冤家亲》在中国曲协、山东省文化厅举办的“欢歌笑语”曲艺大赛中荣获“乌金杯”表演一等奖。1995年，表演的山东琴书《魂系桃花庄》在中国曲协举办的第二届中国曲艺节中荣获牡丹奖。2010年，表演的山东琴书《一只咸菜罐》在山东省第六届小品曲艺大赛中荣获一等奖。魏务良在工作之余还不忘培养新一代传承人，他举办山东琴书传习班，经常为青年演员讲述山东琴书的发展史和演唱风格，培养出的青年演员在曲艺大赛中多次获奖。

Wei Wuliang—Inheritor of Shandong Qinshu

Wei Wuliang, male, born in Jinan, Shandong Province in 1956, is a first-class actor of Jinan Quyi Troupe.

Shandong Qinshu originated in Southwest Shandong in the early Qing Dynasty. In its early stage, it was a form of folk singing for self-entertainment. There were many amateur classes and clubs, which formed the singing custom of annual festivals. The musical structure is a form of syntheses, with *The Legend of White Snake* as the main repertoire, and more than 300 pieces of music are used in conjunction. In the late Guangxu Reign of the Qing Dynasty, due to the famine, Liu Laoji of Yuncheng and Li Fengxing of Jinxiang went to Shanghai to become the first professional artists. Gradually, the form of many people singing were changed into two or three people singing and playing musical instruments, such as urheen, dulcimer, and etc. by themselves. The music structure has developed into the main interpolation form with the dominant "old six main songs".

In 1978, Wei Wuliang began to follow the famous South Shandong Qinshu artists Li Ruoliang and Li Xiangyun to learn to sing the South Shandong Qinshu repertoire *Love Hate* (Shuiman Jinshan in Chinese Pinyin), *Kou Zhun Refuses the Banquet, Pinch a Guy* and *Partridge Days*. In 1981, Wei Wuliang formally took Li Xiangyun as his teacher to learn the singing methods and performing skills of South Shandong Qinshu.

In the process of learning Shandong Qinshu, Wei Wuliang analyzed its characteristics in singing style, charm, pronunciation, measures, scenery setting and performance, and etc. The essences of South Shandong Qinshu and North Qinshu are integrated into an organic whole by him, which offers the opportunity of mutual study and reference.

Wei Wuliang's singing tunes and Shandong Qinshu programs have been awarded prizes many times in the whole country and in Shandong Province. In 1986, the Shandong Qinshu *Closer Relatives* he performed won the bronze prize of the Ministry of Culture. In 1989, his performance of Shandong Qinshu *Enemy Marriage* won the first prize of "Wujin Cup" performance in the "Joy and Laughter" Quyi Competition held by the Chinese Ballad Singers Association and Shandong Provincial Department of Culture and Tourism. In 1995, his performance of Shandong Qinshu *Soul in Peach Blossom Village* won the Peony Award in the 2nd Chinese Quyi Festival held by the Chinese Quyi Association. In 2010, the performance of Shandong Qinshu *A Salted Vegetable Can* won the first prize in the 6th Shandong Sketch and Quyi Competition. In addition to his works, Wei Wuliang has not forgotten to train a new generation of inheritors. He holds a seminar on Shandong Qinshu. He often tells young actors the development history and singing style of Shandong Qinshu. The young actors and actresses trained by him won prizes in many opera competitions.

山东琴书传承人——杨珀

杨珀，女，1963年出生，山东济南人，济南曲艺团国家一级演员，享国务院政府特殊津贴。

山东琴书发源于鲁西南菏泽地区，是在明清俗曲基础上形成的以联曲体为主的一种曲艺形式，是我国曲牌体曲种中发展最为成熟完备的曲艺形式之一。随着时间的推移，山东琴书发展出了东、南、北三路艺术流派，三路流派风格迥异，各具特色。

1978年，杨珀考入济南市曲艺团从事曲艺表演工作，跟随山东琴书（北路）传承人姚忠贤学习。她在学习中注重继承传统演唱技法，较为全面系统地掌握了山东琴书（北路）的演唱特点、传统唱段，并在演出中加以实践。在与姚忠贤老师多年的合作演出中共同努力，把山东琴书这一传统曲目打造成为现代观众喜闻乐见的曲艺形式。

杨珀在多年的演出实践活动中积累了丰富的经验，形成了自己独特的演唱风格。她在继承传统的基础上大胆创新，创造性地在山东琴书的音乐及唱腔中植入民歌、戏曲、姊妹曲种等元素，使山东琴书的曲调更加丰富。杨珀在表演及表现形式上注重强化人物塑造，强调个性化和真实感，增加了幽默对白，更富节奏感，并突破单一坐唱的形式，使山东琴书这一传统民间艺术在保留其原有特色的前提下焕发了新生机，让更多的人特别是青年观众接受和喜爱。

杨珀高度注重后备人才的培养，在济南市曲艺团教授青年演员，在济南非物质文化遗产基地从事琴书教学工作。她在教授学生之余还积极参加各种活动，2009年起参加“齐鲁文化讲坛”活动，先后赴清华大学、北京大学、中山大学等100余所全国著名高校，传播山东琴书艺术。多年来，杨珀获得了多个奖项。1990年，参加全国曲艺大赛，演唱山东琴书《冤家亲》并荣获表演二等奖。2000年，参加中国曲艺牡丹奖大赛，演唱山东琴书《生灵叹》并荣获金奖 。2010年，在法国巴黎获中国曲艺节卢浮银奖。

Yang Po—Inheritor of Shandong Qinshu

Yang Po, female, born in Jinan, Shandong Province in 1963, is a first-class actress of Jinan Quyi Troupe. She enjoys special allowance from the State Council.

Shandong Qinshu originated in Heze area of Southwest Shandong. It is a form of music art with a form of syntheses based on the folk music of the Ming and Qing Dynasties. It is one of the most mature and complete forms of folk music in China. With the passage of time, Shandong Qinshu has developed three art schools: East, South and North, which have different styles and characteristics.

In 1978, Yang Po was admitted to Jinan Quyi Troupe to work as an actress, and was apprenticed to Yao Zhongxian, the inheritor of Shandong Qinshu (North). She paid attention to inheriting the traditional singing skills in her study, had a comprehensive and systematic grasp of the singing characteristics, traditional arias of Shandong Qinshu (North) and practiced them in the performance. She has worked together with Yao Zhongxian for many years to make Shandong Qinshu, a traditional musical repertoire, a popular form of music for modern audiences.

Yang Po has accumulated rich experience during many years of practice and formed her own unique singing style. On the basis of inheriting the tradition, she boldly innovates and creatively implants folk songs, operas and sister songs into the music and singing tunes of Shandong Qinshu, which enriches its tunes. Yang Po highlights strengthening the characterization, and emphasizes individuality and authenticity. She has increased the sense of humor and rhythm, and broke through the single sitting and singing form, so that Shandong Qinshu, a traditional folk art, is revitalized while retaining its original characteristics, and is accepted and appreciated by

more people, especially young audiences.

Yang Po attaches great importance to the training of reserve talents. She teaches young actors in Jinan Quyi Troupe and is engaged in Qinshu teaching in Jinan Intangible Cultural Heritage Base. She has also actively participated in various activities besides teaching students. Since 2009, she has participated in the Qilu Cultural Forum. She has been to more than 100 famous universities in China, such as Tsinghua University, Peking University and Sun Yat-sen University, to disseminate the art of Shandong Qinshu. Over the years, Yang Po has won many awards. In 1990, she participated in the National Quyi Competition and won the second prize for performing Shandong Qinshu *Enemy Marriage*. In 2000, she participated in the Chinese Quyi Peony Prize Competition, and won the gold prize for her performance of Shandong Qinshu *The Wonder of Life*. In 2010, she won the Louvre Silver Award at the Paris China Quyi Festival in Paris, France.

山东琴书传承人——李巧莲

李巧莲，女，1950 年出生，山东菏泽人。

山东琴书起源于民间、活跃在民间，是一种百姓喜闻乐见的曲艺形式。山东琴书表演风格独特；语言质朴自然；音乐形式多样，兼有联曲、主插、板式变化等形式；曲目数量多，造诣高，富有地方特色，深受底层百姓喜爱。

1968 年，李巧莲跟随成武曲艺队的吴爱云学习山东琴书。1975 年，师从韩传敬学习山东琴书，后由国家级山东琴书传承人李湘云亲身传授山东琴书技艺。

李巧莲继承了山东琴书优美娟秀、细致委婉、朴素大方、高昂奔放的特点，并在长期的艺术实践中，形成了自己独有的演唱风格。她的手、眼、身、法、步、口基本功扎实，特别是眼神的运用独具特色。她在演唱中的可塑性很强，能快能慢。慢者，慢而不散，字字落地；快者，快而不乱，赶板夺词。在语言方面，她的语言生动、精练，富有意境，雅俗共赏；在演唱方面，她擅长塑造人物形象，刻画人物准确细腻，吐字清晰，声情并茂，感人至深；在形体表演方面，她从剧中人物出发，精心研究人物之后再细致地设计表演程式，塑造了许多性格鲜明的艺术形象。

李巧莲多次参加全国、省、市会演，获得了许多荣誉。1989 年，表演的山东琴书《回娘家》获山东省曲艺大赛优秀节目奖。2000 年，表演的山东琴书《扒墙头》获山东省曲艺大赛三等奖。2013 年，表演的山东琴书《亲上亲》参加全国十艺节曲艺优秀节目展演并荣获优秀表演奖。李巧莲还主动传承山东琴书，1998~2001 年，在菏泽公关学校和中原艺校任山东琴书教师期间，先后培养了多名优秀学生。2004 年至今，被菏泽学院音乐系特聘为山东琴书教授，从事山东琴书教学工作，在大学领域开辟了传承山东琴书的平台，使山东琴书得到了有效的传承和发扬。

Li Qiaolian—Inheritor of Shandong Qinshu

Li Qiaolian, female, was born in Heze, Shandong Province in 1950.

Shandong Qinshu is originated from the folk, active in the folk, and is a popular form of folk music well received by people. Shandong Qinshu has a unique performing style. It is in simple and natural language, diverse musical forms, including comics, main interludes, plate changes, and etc. It has a large number of repertoires, high attainments, rich local characteristics, and is much appreciated by the common people.

In 1968, Li Qiaolian followed Wu Aiyun of Chengwu Quyi Team to study Shandong Qinshu. In 1975, she learned Shandong Qinshu from Han Chuanjing, and then was taught the skills by Li Xiangyun personally, a national inheritor of Shandong Qinshu.

Li Qiaolian inherited the characteristics of Shandong Qinshu like beauty, gracefulness, meticulousness and euphemisticness, simplicity and generosity, high and unrestrained nature, and formed her own unique singing style in the long-term artistic practice. Her basic skills of hands, eyes, body, mode, steps and mouth are solid, especially her unique use of eyes. She is very plastic in singing, able to be fast or slow. Slow but not scattered, her words are emphasized; fast but not disorderly, her words catch up with the rhythm. In terms of language, her language is vivid, refined, full of artistic conception, elegant and popular. In terms of singing, she is good at portraying characters accurately and delicately. She articulates clearly, full of voice and emotion, touching the audience deeply. In terms of body performance, she starts from the characters in the play, carefully studies the characters, then carefully designs the performance program, and shapes many artistic images with distinct personality.

Li Qiaolian has participated in many national, provincial and municipal performances and won many honors. In 1989, the performance of Shandong Qinshu *On the Way to the Wife's Parents* won the excellent program award of Shandong Quyi Competition. In 2000, Shandong Qinshu *Climbing the Wall* won the third prize of Shandong Quyi Competition. In 2013, Shandong Qinshu *Closer Relatives* won the excellent performance award at the National Ten Arts Festival. Li Qiaolian also took the initiative to inherit Shandong Qinshu. From 1998 to 2001, she trained many excellent students in Heze Public Relations School and Zhongyuan Art School as a teacher of Shandong Qinshu. Since 2004, she has been specially appointed as a professor of Shandong Qinshu by the Music Department of Heze University to teach Shandong Qinshu, which has provided a platform for inheriting Shandong Qinshu in the University field. She has effectively inherited and developed Shandong Qinshu.

山东琴书传承人——毕美

毕美，女，1960年出生，山东菏泽人，菏泽市曲艺家协会副主席。

山东琴书早期是自娱自乐的民间演唱形式，有着300余年的历史。清末民初，山东琴书进入鼎盛发展时期，进而发展出了以商业兴为代表的“东路琴书”、以邓九如为代表的“北路琴书”和鲁西南原产地的“南路琴书”三大流派。南路琴书主要流行于鲁西南及周边省市，是琴书的发源地，在艺人数量、器乐演奏水平、曲书目数量方面均具有较大影响。

1975年，毕美参加成武县文化馆宣传队，跟随老师学习唱歌，为以后学习山东琴书奠定了基础。1977年，她参加菏泽地区曲艺队，正式学习山东琴书演唱，在王振刚、胡化山等南路琴书艺人的教授下，很快就担任了山东琴书的主要演唱任务。在演唱工作期间，她还不断提升自己，经常向优秀民间艺人学习传统唱段、唱腔、曲牌，努力提高自己的演唱水平。

琴书要求演员不光要唱得好，还要精通一件或多件乐器。因此，毕美学唱的同时还兼学扬琴和古筝演奏。她认真学习研究每一个唱段、每一句唱腔、每一个曲牌，认真吸收老艺人的精华。正因如此，她在演唱中才能准确、细腻地刻画人物。她的唱腔韵味醇厚，嗓音明亮，吐词咬字清晰，字正腔圆，形成了自己独特的演唱风格。

2003年，毕美组建了菏泽说唱团，培养了一批学员。此外，她不定期为菏泽学院学生授课辅导，以延续山东琴书艺术的传承。从艺几十年来，毕美还多次参加全国曲艺大赛，受到了专家及同行的好评。1981年，演唱的山东琴书《大林还家》参加全国优秀曲艺节目演出，获文化部演出一等奖。1984年，演唱的山东琴书《重聚梁山》，参加山东省中长篇书会，获省文化厅、省文联演出一等奖。

Bi Mei—Inheritor of Shandong Qinshu

Bi Mei, female, born in 1960, is a native of Heze, Shandong Province. She is the vice president of Heze Quyi Artists Association.

Shandong Qinshu was a folk singing form of self-entertainment in its early stage, with a history of more than 300 years. In the late Qing Dynasty and early Republic of China, Shandong Qinshu entered a period of flourishing development, and then developed into "East Qinshu" represented by commercial prosperity, and "North Qinshu" represented by Deng Jiuru and "South Qinshu" originated in southwest Shandong. South Shandong Qinshu is popular mainly in southwest Shandong and its surrounding provinces and cities, the birthplace of Qinshu. South Shandong Qinshu has great influence on the number of artists, the level of instrumental music performance and the number of tunes.

In 1975, Bi Mei participated in the propaganda team of Chengwu Cultural Museum, following the teacher to learn singing, which laid the foundation for future study of Shandong Qinshu. In 1977, she participated in Heze Regional Quyi Team and began officially to study Shandong Qinshu singing. Under the supervision of professors Wang Zhengang and Hu Huashan, she soon took up the main singing task of Shandong Qinshu. In her singing career, she also constantly upgraded herself, often learning traditional arias, singing tunes and tune names from outstanding folk artists, and striving to improve her singing level.

Qinshu require actors not only to sing well, but also to be proficient in one or more instruments. Therefore, while singing, Bi Mei also learned to play the dulcimer and zither. She seriously studied and researched every aria, every song, every tune, and carefully absorbed the essence of the old artists. Because of this, she can accurately and delicately portray the characters in her singing. Her vocal charm is mellow, her voice volume is bright, and her tune intonation is clear, hence developing her own unique singing style.

In 2003, Bi Mei set up Heze Rap Troupe and trained a group of students. In addition, she regularly taught and coached students of Heze College in order to continue the inheritance of Shandong Qinshu art. In the past decades, Bi Mei has participated in the National Quyi Competition many times, and has been praised by experts and colleagues. In 1981, with Shandong Qinshu *Dalin Returned Home*, she participated in the National Excellent Quyi Performance and was awarded the first prize by the Ministry of Culture. In 1984, the Shandong Qinshu *Rejuvenating on Liang Mountain* starred by her, was performed in the Shandong Medium-length Book Fair, and was awarded the first performance prize by Shandong Provincial Department of Culture and Tourism and Shandong Federation of Literature and Art Circles.

山东快书传承人——高洪胜

高洪胜，男，1954 年出生，河南人，国家一级演员。

山东快书是以一个人表演一部书（如《武松传》），塑造一个形象（如武松）而形成的韵诵类曲艺品种。山东快书原名“武老二”，演唱者俗称“唱武老二的”。直到 1949 年，著名快书表演艺术家高元钧才将其正式定名为“山东快书”。其起源于清道光年间，20 世纪 50 年代进入了鼎盛时期，逐渐出现了以高元钧为代表的“高派”、以杨立德为代表的“杨派”、以于传宾为代表的“于派”三个流派。山东快书的总体风格豪迈粗犷，幽默滑稽，具有独特韵味。

高洪胜从小受家庭艺术的熏陶，自幼随父山东快书大师高元钧学习山东快书，在父亲的严格教授下深得山东快书的艺术精髓，在上学期间就经常演出，为其以后的艺术生涯打下了坚实的基础。参军后，高洪胜也一直从事艺术工作，曾进入解放军艺术学院深造，经过长期的艺术实践，其表演风格逐渐成熟。

高洪胜的表演准确自然，刻画人物鲜活；语言准确流畅，幽默雅俗恰当；吐字归音考究，节奏扎实明快；形体律动优美，台风潇洒自如。他的表演涉猎广泛，演唱传统作品时，能保持经典原貌，原汁原味，严格规范；表演现代作品时，能不断创新进步，新颖自然独特，具有时代美感。

高洪胜懂理论，精教学；能创作，善表演。他教授出了一批山东快书演员，为山东快书的继承和发展做出了重要贡献。他创作、表演的山东快书《军神》荣获全军第五届文艺会演创作、表演一等奖；创作、表演的山东快书《陈毅吃请》荣获全军第六届文艺会演表演一等奖、创作二等奖；创作、表演的山东快书《许世友一跪毛泽东》获第五届中国曲艺牡丹奖表演奖。

Gao Hongsheng—Inheritor of Shandong Clapper Ballad

Gao Hongsheng, male, born in Henan Province in 1954, is a national first-class actor.

Shandong Clapper Ballad is a kind of rhyming folk art which is formed by a person performing a book (such as *Biography of Wu Song*) and creating an image (such as Wu Song). The original name of Shandong Clapper Ballad was "Wu Lao'er", and the singer was commonly known as "Wu Lao'er Singer". It was until 1949 that Gao Yuanjun, a famous Clapper Ballad performing artist, formally named it Shandong Clapper Ballad. It originated in the Daoguang Reign of the Qing Dynasty, and entered its heyday in the 1950s. Gradually, there emerged three genres: Gao genre represented by Gao Yuanjun, Yang genre represented by Yang Lide, and Yu genre represented by Yu Chuanbin. The overall style of Shandong Clapper Ballad is bold and rugged, humorous and funny, with unique charm.

Gao Hongsheng was influenced by family art since childhood. He started to learn Shandong Clapper Ballad from his father Gao Yuanjun, a master of Shandong Clapper Ballad, since childhood and under his father's strict teaching, he acquired the artistic essence of Shandong Clapper Ballad. He often performed in school, laying a solid foundation for his later artistic career. After joining the army, Gao Hongsheng had also been engaged in art work. He entered People's Liberation Army Academy of Arts for further study. After a long period of artistic practice, his performance style has been gradually becoming mature.

Gao Hongsheng's performance is accurate and natural, vivid in characterization, accurate and fluent in language, elegant and vulgar in humor, exquisite in pronunciation, solid and lively in rhythm, graceful in body and natural in stage style. His performance covers a wide range of subjects. When singing traditional works, he can maintain the original classical appearance, original taste and strict norms. When performing modern works, he can constantly innovate and progress, thus making his performance novel, natural and unique, and possess the aesthetic feeling of the times.

Gao Hongsheng knows theory and excels in teaching. He is creative and performs well. He has taught a number of Shandong Clapper Ballad actors and made important contributions to the inheritance and development of Shandong Clapper Ballad. His Shandong Clapper Ballad Army God won the first prize in creation and performance of the 5th PLA Literary and Art Festival. His Shandong Clapper Ballad *Chen Yi's Invitation to Dinner* won the first prize of performance and the second prize of creation in the 6th PLA Literary and Art Performance. And his Shandong Clapper Ballad Xu Shiyou's One Kneeling before Mao Zedong won the performance award of Peony Award in the 5th Chinese Quyi Festival.

山东琴书传承人——何淑玲

何淑玲，女，1946 年出生，山东郓城人，菏泽市民间曲艺家，菏泽市首批乡土文艺人才。

清雍正年间，山东琴书发源于鲁西南地区。光绪年间，鲁西南地区灾荒连年，一批擅长“小曲子”的艺人开始下海卖艺，他们改进唱腔和伴奏，充实书目，促进了山东琴书的蓬勃发展。清末民初，涌现出一大批琴书名家，山东琴书进入鼎盛时期。中华人民共和国成立后，山东琴书艺人也一直活跃在各种曲艺演出中，山东琴书逐渐发展成为成熟完备的曲艺形式，在曲牌体曲种中占据一席之地。

1963 年，何淑玲考入郓城县曲艺队，开始学习山东琴书。1964 年，在县文化馆组织的曲牌挖掘培训班学习。1969 年，跟随曲艺家李素云学习唱腔和曲牌。1974 年，参加菏泽文化局举办的培训班，提高了自己的演唱水平。2010 起，担任郓城县曲艺团业务团长。

何淑玲熟练掌握 130 余种曲牌，演唱的曲牌以上合调、凤阳歌、梅花落等为主。她的演唱咬字真切，稳重大方，平易中求韵味；唱腔优美动听，声情并茂，富于变化，并熟练掌握了五种乐器，能自弹自唱。何淑玲的演唱有三个明显特点：一是灵活多变，演唱的作品多数为短篇作品，一般有一二百句，篇幅短小，形式灵活，叫作“唱段”，常常能迅速地反映生活；二是叙述故事时，以第三人称叙述故事为主，辅以必要的进入角色的代言身份，塑造鲜明的艺术形象；三是演绎柔美，富有感染力，擅长言情。

几十年来，何淑玲积极进行创作，作品多次在全国、全省获奖。《樊梨花投唐》获全国曲艺会演二等奖。《女饲养员》《千里送暖》获山东省曲艺会演一等奖。《俺的新家》获中国电视艺术家协会一等奖，并获苏鲁豫皖曲艺会演一等奖。何淑玲在工作的同时，还不忘山东琴书的传承和发展。1997 年以来，她先后培养了多名山东琴书传承人，使诸多山东琴书曲牌得以完整继承，为山东琴书的发展和繁荣做出了贡献。

He Shuling—Inheritor of Shandong Qinshu

He Shuling, female, was born in Yuncheng County, Shandong Province in 1946. She is a folk Quyi artist, and one of the first batch of local literary talents in Heze.

During the Yongzheng Reign of the Qing Dynasty, Shandong Qinshu originated in southwest Shandong. During the Guangxu Reign, a group of artists who were good at "Xiaoquzi" began to make a living as performers. They improved the way of singing and accompaniment, enriched the bibliography and promoted the prosperity of Shandong Qinshu. In the late Qing Dynasty and early Republic of China, a large number of famous Qinshu artists emerged, and Shandong Qinshu entered the heyday. Since the founding of People's Republic of China, Shandong Qinshu artists have been active in various performances. Gradually Shandong Qinshu become a mature and complete form of opera, occupying a place in the genre of Qupai.

In 1963, He Shuling was admitted to Yuncheng County Quyi Team and began to study Shandong Qinshu. In 1964, she took a training course organized by the County Cultural Centre. In 1969, he followed Li Suyun, a Quyi artist, to learn singing aria and Qupai. In 1974, she attended a training course held by Heze Cultural Bureau, which improved her singing level. Since 2010, she has been the business leader of Yuncheng County Quyi Troupe.

He Shuling proficiently mastered more than 130 Qupais, mainly including "Shanghe Tune" "Fengyang Songs" "Plum Blossom Falls", and so on. Her singing is genuine, stable and generous, seeking charm in the plain. Her tune is beautiful and pleasant, full of changes. She is skilled in five kinds of musical instruments, and is able to play and sing at the same time. He Shuling's singing has three distinct characteristics. Firstly, she is flexible and changeable. Most of her works are short, usually in one or two hundred sentences, short in length and flexible in form, often reflecting life quickly. Secondly, when narrating stories, she mainly adopts the third person point of view, supplemented by the necessary spokesman, to create distinct artistic images. Thirdly, the performance is soft, appealing and good at expressing feelings.

He Shuling has been actively creating works for decades, and her works have won national and provincial prizes for many times. *Fan Lihua Surrender to the Tang Dynasty* won the second prize of the National Quyi Performance. *Female Raiser* and *To Send Warmth from Thousands of Miles Away* won the first prize of Shandong Quyi Performance. *My New Home* won the first prize of China TV Art Association and the first prize of Jiangsu, Shandong, Henan and Anhui Quyi Joint Performance. He Shuling, while working, has not forgotten the inheritance and development of Shandong Qinshu. Since 1997, she has trained many inheritors of Shandong Qinshu successively, so that many Shandong Qinshu Qupais could be completely inherited, which contributed to the development and prosperity of Shandong Qinshu.

山东渔鼓传承人——刘炳金

刘炳金，男，1949 年出生，山东济宁人。

渔鼓最初名为“道情”，原为道教宣讲经卷活动时所唱的一种道曲，是一种源于道教而又逐渐世俗化的民间曲艺形式，因用渔鼓和简板作为伴奏乐器，所以叫作“渔鼓”。流行于山东境内的道情书，通称为“山东渔鼓”。山东渔鼓演出形式较为简单，无弦索伴奏，不用桌椅道具，多为一人单挑，左手持简板、抱渔鼓，右手击鼓兼做手势，渔鼓还可兼做道具使用。山东渔鼓的数目较多，有《闹天宫》《小秃闹房》等 30 余种段儿书及《红心江》《李双喜借年》等 20 余部中长篇书。

1963 年，刘炳金拜师渔鼓艺人黄永胜先生学艺，学习渔鼓。1965 年，加入嘉祥县文艺工作队，表演曲艺节目。1975 年，进金乡县四平调剧团，到农村表演渔鼓。1980 年，被调到地区吕剧团专职演戏。1987 年，调离剧团后，参加济宁市曲艺家协会，重操旧业。经过多年的演出，刘炳金的表演和创作水平均得到了很大的提高。

刘炳金的腔韵自然，吐字清晰，追求高雅、庄重却又不失风趣，保持了浓厚的乡土气息。他的唱腔大开大合，开张处宽广有力，细腻处婉转入微，主张老渔鼓新唱法，在尊重传统的基础上，大胆革新。他在表演上主张曲艺戏剧化，注重故事情节的表演和人物形象的展示，不局限在语言的描写和唱腔的表现上。刘炳金还积极进行剧目创作，创作了一大批反映时代精神的新剧目。

多年来，刘炳金一直从事山东渔鼓的教学工作，在济宁市多个小学进行课外教授，培养渔鼓优秀人才。他还积极参加各种演出活动。1995 年，演唱的山东渔鼓《孟母三迁》获山东省曲艺邀请赛表演一等奖。1997 年，演唱的山东渔鼓《春天的故事》获鲁西南五地市曲艺比赛一等奖。2001 年，表演的山东渔鼓《断机教子》在全国第十一届群星奖曲艺比赛中获金奖。

Liu Bingjin—Inheritor of Shandong Fishing Drum

Liu Bingjin, male, was born in Jining, Shandong Province in 1949.

The earliest name of Fishing Drum was "Dao Qing". It was originally a kind of Taoist melody sung during Taoist propaganda activities. It is a folk music form originating from Taoism and was gradually secularized. It is called Fishing Drum because it uses Fishing Drum and simple clapper as accompaniment instruments. Dao Qing popular in Shandong Province is commonly known as "Shandong Fishing Drum". The performance form of Shandong Fishing Drum is relatively simple, with no string accompaniment, no tables and chairs, and mostly one performer, whose left hand holds simple clapper and Fishing Drum, and right hand beats the drum and makes gestures. Fishing Drum can also be used as props. There are many Fishing Drum tunes in Shandong Province, including more than 30 short pieces such as *Uproar in Heaven, Xiao Tu Nao Fang*, and more than 20 medium and long pieces, such as *Hong Xin River, Li Shuangxi Borrowing Year.*

In 1963, Liu Bingjin was apprenticed to Mr. Huang Yongsheng, a Fishing Drum artist, and studied Fishing Drum. In 1965, he joined the Literature and Art Troupe of Jiaxiang County to perform Quyi programmes. In 1975, he went to the Siping Opera Troupe of Jinxiang County to perform Fishing Drum in the countryside. In 1980, he was transferred to the local Lü Opera Troupe as a full-time performer. In 1987, after leaving the troupe, he joined Jining Quyi Artists Association and worked as a Quyi performer again. Through years of performance, Liu Bingjin's performance level and creative level both have been greatly improved.

Liu Bingjin's style of natural rhyme, clear pronunciation, pursuit of elegance, solemnity with humor, maintain a strong local flavor. His aria is open and close, wide and powerful, delicate and subtle, combining the old drum tradition and new singing method, and boldly making innovations on the basis of respecting tradition. In his performance, he advocated the dramatization of the opera, focusing on the plots and the display of characters, instead of confining to the description of language and the performance of singing. Liu Bingjin also actively created plays and produced a large number of new plays reflecting the spirit of the times.

Over the years, Liu Bingjin has been engaged in the teaching of Fishing Drum in Shandong Province. He has taught Fishing Drum in extracurricular time in many primary schools in Jining City, and has cultivated excellent talents of Fishing Drum. He has also actively participated in various performances. In 1995, Shandong Fishing Drum programme *Meng Mu San Qian* starred by him won the first prize in Shandong Invitational Competition of Quyi. In 1997, Shandong Fishing Drum programme *The Story of Spring* starred by him won the first prize in the Quyi Competition of Five Cities in Southwest Shandong. In 2001, his Shandong Fishing Drum programme *Duan Ji Jiao Zi* won the gold medal in the 11th National Star Award Quyi Competition.

傳承人

传统体育、游艺与杂技
Traditional Sports, Entertainment and Acrobatics

莒县查拳传承人——庄会升

庄会升，男，1951 年出生，山东日照人，莒县武术运动协会主席。

莒县查拳属于“杨式—萧派”查拳，昆仑派，查密尔小架子拳，内容以纯格斗为主。莒县查拳按照“先天伏羲八卦主生，后天文王八卦主克，双数主养，单数主杀”的原理行拳，动作组合用一、三、五、七、九这五个单数。具有形神兼备、结构严谨、功架整齐、虚实分明、迅猛有力、攻防有致、清晰连贯的特点。在动作上，莒县查拳具有工整、流畅、轻灵、飘逸、纵达、雄浑、缜密、端严的“查拳品”，在实战技击方面形成了出手疾、回手快、触发寸劲，虚打实上、避实就虚，明拳暗腿、手脚并用，组合连击的风格。

庄会升 6 岁就在莒县清真寺跟随萧羲之习武，习拳 26 年，是萧羲之先生的关门弟子。自 1976 年萧羲之去世后，作为“杨式—萧派”查拳的关门弟子，庄会升一直谨遵师父“分文不取地将查拳这一武术瑰宝传承下去”的教诲，白天打工，晚上在家义务授徒。

庄会升努力探索，创新莒县查拳套路。在融会贯通各路查拳特长的基础上，他悉心探索，充分发挥查拳“手似两扇门，全凭足打人”的特点，创编的三路蛟龙拳，每一拳路都注重箭弹等动作，并将五形动作融入查拳，龙行虎步，疾如鹰、起如猿、立如鹤，具有刚烈雄壮、舒展大方的特点。

在努力创新莒县查拳套路之余，庄会升还勤于研究，著述丰富，同时积极参加各种比赛。他于 2012 年获日照市武术比赛“单刀对枪”“钢鞭”一等奖，2013 年获第 13 届全国子午门少林学校武术争霸赛“哪吒枪”金牌。近年来，庄会升在市、县非物质文化遗产保护中心的帮助下，成立了莒县查拳研究会，组织了“查拳进校园”活动，为千余名学生普及查拳知识，教授查拳动作，为莒县查拳传承做出了重要贡献。

Zhuang Huisheng—Inheritor of Ju Zha Quan

Zhuang Huisheng, male, born in Rizhao, Shandong Province in 1951, is the President of Ju County Martial Arts Sports Association.

Ju Zha Quan belongs to the "Yang Type-Xiao Faction", Kunlun Genre, the content of which is mainly pure fighting. It is characterized by vividness in terms of both form and spirit, rigorous structure, neat work frame, clear virtual-real distinction, rapidity and forcefulness, delicate attack and defense, clarity and coherence. In action, Ju Zha Quan has neat, fluent, light, elegant, lenient, vigorous, meticulous and rigorous "Zha Quan motions". In real fights, it has formed its own unique style.

At the age of 6, Zhuang Huisheng followed Xiao Xizhi in his martial arts practice at Ju County. He practiced boxing for 26 years. He was Xiao Xizhi's last disciple. Since Xiao Xizhi's death in 1976, as the last disciple of "Yang Type-Xiao Faction" Zha Quan, Zhuang Huisheng has been following the Master's teaching that "Zha Quan is a treasure of martial arts that should be inherited without taking any money". He worked during the day and taught his apprentices at home at night voluntarily.

Zhuang Huisheng has made great efforts to explore and innovate Ju Zha Quan. On the basis of integrating the expertise of different factions of Zha Quan, he explored thoroughly and gave full play to the characteristics of *Zhaquan* that "hands are like two doors; hitting person depends all by feet".

In addition to innovating Ju Zha Quan routine, Zhuang Huisheng was also diligent in research. He has written many books and he actively participated in various competitions. He won the first prize of "Single-Knife Versus Gun" and "Steel Whip" in Rizhao Martial Arts Competition in 2012 and the gold medal of "Nezha Gun" in the 13th National Martial Arts Competition of Meridian Shaolin School in 2013. In recent years, with the help of the Intangible Cultural Heritage Protection Centers of Rizhao and Ju County, Zhuang Huisheng established the Ju Zha Quan Research Association, organized the "Zha Quan Entering Campus" activities and made an important contribution to the inheritance of Ju Zha Quan.

鸳鸯螳螂拳传承人——孙日成

孙日成，男，1967 年出生，山东青岛人，齐鲁文化之星。

鸳鸯螳螂拳有着独特的韵味和特点，取“鸳鸯”之意，一为阴阳理法内外双修，二为拳法动作左右对称，取“螳螂”之名，不在象形而重在取螳螂迅猛和手法精妙多变之意。鸳鸯螳螂拳动作古朴浑厚，技法丰富，结构严谨，衔接巧妙，技击性强。习练以内气为源，腰背力量为基础，内外结合；套路中每组招式左右手组合练习，克服了一般拳术中只注重右手单面而左手较弱的缺点，在实战中左右手绵延相继，开合有续，攻其不备，以占据优势。

孙日成自幼随父习鸳鸯螳螂拳，是鸳鸯螳螂拳第五代传承人。自 1988 年起，孙日成开始搜集整理关于鸳鸯螳螂拳的各种材料，为鸳鸯螳螂拳的研究奠定了基础，2005 年成立青岛鸳鸯螳螂拳武馆，教习拳法。2008 年 4 月至今，孙日成一直致力于鸳鸯螳螂拳的传承工作，开设了多期公益传习班，在青岛市掀起了学习武术的热潮。

孙日成在对外交流与传播上做了大量工作。2010 年起被聘为牛顿国际公学客座教授，曾为美国贝特蒙大学的教授和学生讲解“了解中国传统文化，学习中国功夫”的课程，多次参加由青岛市文化部门组织的国际交流活动，为中国鸳鸯螳螂拳走出国门打下了坚实的基础。

2006 年，孙日成在国际香港螳螂拳邀请赛中获得“两金一银”；2012 年，被山东省委组织部和宣传部授予“齐鲁文化之星”称号。2013 年 4 月，孙日成带领中华鸳鸯门派文武会馆代表队参加香港国际武术比赛，共获得 36 枚金牌、22 枚银牌、18 枚铜牌及 2 个团体第一名。

Sun Richeng—Inheritor of Mandarin Duck and Mantis Boxing

Sun Richeng, male, born in Qingdao, Shandong Province in 1967, is the Star of Qilu Culture.

Mandarin Duck and Mantis Boxing has its unique charm and characteristics. It takes the meanings of mandarin duck at two aspects: one is the internal and external double-training according to Yin and Yang principles; the other is the left-right symmetry of boxing movements. It also takes the name of mantis not for pictograph, but focusing on the meaning of quick, violent, subtle and changeable manners of the mantis. Mandarin Duck and Mantis Boxing is simple and honest, with rich skills, rigorous structure, skillful cohesion, and strong attack power.

Sun Richeng learned Mandarin Duck and Mantis Boxing from his father since he was a child. He is the fifth-generation inheritor of Mandarin Duck and Mantis Boxing. In 1988, Sun Richeng began to collect and sort out materials about Mandarin Duck and Mantis Boxing, which laid a foundation for his later study. In 2005, Qingdao Mandarin Duck and Mantis Boxing Museum was established to teach boxing. Since April, 2008, Sun Richeng has been devoting himself to the inheritance of Mandarin Duck and Mantis Boxing.

Sun Richeng has done a lot of work in international exchange and communication. Since 2010, he has been employed as a visiting professor of Newton International School. He has lectured on "Understanding Chinese Traditional Culture and Learning Chinese Kungfu" to professors and students of Belmont University in the United States. He has participated in international exchange events organized by Qingdao cultural departments for many times, laying a solid foundation for Chinese Mandarin Duck and Mantis Boxing going abroad.

In 2006, Sun Richeng won two gold medals and one silver medal in the International Mantis Boxing Invitational Competition in Hong Kong. In 2012, he was awarded the title of Star of Qilu Culture by the Organizational Department and Propaganda Department of Shandong Provincial Committee. In April 2013, Sun Richeng led the Chinese Mantis School Team to participate in the Hong Kong International Martial Arts Competition. In this competition, the Chinese Mantis School Team won 36 gold medals, 22 silver medals, 18 bronze medals and won the first place of two team competitions.

文圣拳传承人——宋连洪

宋连洪，男，1953 年出生，山东汶上人，文圣拳第三代传承人。

文圣拳以古代阴阳五行变化的原理为拳艺指南，由文功和武功两部分组成，文功即静功，武功即动功。文功主要是以调息、入静、养气、练意为功法拳法之根本，方式有静坐、侧卧、仰卧、站立等。武功，主要是练形求法，动作中讲究阴阳变化，刚柔舒展，伸筋拔骨，以意行气，以气促力，气到力到，意、气、力相结合，方法上讲究沾、粘、连、随、挤、跟、靠、打等。

宋连洪生于文圣拳世家，自幼随祖父宋传平、父亲宋如一习武，其祖父宋传平对文圣拳武功套路逐一定架、定式，以圣贤之心领悟拳法之道，取“武中文功，武以文成”之意定名“文圣拳”。其父系统地掌握了内外功的套路技艺及功法理论，多年来一直致力于业余武术教学及文圣拳健身理论的研究。

宋连洪在长期的学习中深得父亲和祖父的真传，并在长期的艺术实践中形成了自己独有的艺术风格。他精通文圣九路梅花大刀、六合大枪、跃步奇枪、文圣剑，尤其擅长本拳散手，在原有的拳术技击基础上有所创新，一招多解、一招多用，比如文圣拳的盘肘式主攻敌手下盘。宋连洪根据动作特点将盘肘式拓展为攻击敌手上、中、下盘，丰富了传统招式在实战中的应用。

宋连洪多次参加全国、省、市武术比赛并多次获得奖项。1986 年，宋连洪参加全国武术观摩交流大会并荣获雄狮奖；1988 年，被济宁市武术运动协会评为市级武术教练员；2011 年，在山东梁山参加全国子午门争霸赛并获金奖。多年来，宋连洪收徒 30 余人，培养了多名文圣拳爱好者，为文圣拳的传承和发展做了大量工作。

Song Lianhong—Inheritor of Wensheng Boxing

Song Lianhong, male, born in Wenshang, Shandong in 1953, is the third-generation inheritor of Wensheng Boxing.

Wensheng Boxing was guided by the principle of invisible change of Yin and Yang in ancient times. It consists of *Wengong* and *Wugong*. *Wengong* is static and *Wugong* is dynamic. *Wengong* is mainly based on breathing adjustment, tranquility, *Qi* nourishment and spirit accumulation. The ways of *Wengong* include sitting, side lying, supine and standing. *Wugong* is mainly to make shape and seek method. In action, it focuses on *Yin* and *Yang* changes, rigidity and flexibility, stretching tendons and pulling bones. We use the spirit to promote *Qi*, use *Qi* to promote strength effectively, and combine the spirit, *Qi*, and strength together. In method, we should pay attention to staining, sticking, joining, linking, squeezing, following, relying, fighting and so on.

Song Lianhong was born in a family of Wensheng Boxing. He practiced martial arts with his grandfather Song Chuanping and his father Song Ruyi. His grandfather Song Chuanping determined the pattern and frame of martial arts routine of Wensheng Boxing one after another, comprehended the way of martial arts with the heart of a sage, and took the ideology of "*Wen* merits in *Wu* and *Wu is* completed by *Wen*" to name the boxing as Wensheng Boxing. His father systematically grasps the skills and theories of both internal and external skills, and has been devoted to amateur martial arts teaching and the research of Wensheng Boxing fitness theory for many years.

Song Lianhong acquired the essence of Wensheng Boxing from his father and grandfather in his long-term study, and formed his own unique artistic style in his long-term artistic practice. He is proficient in Wensheng Nine Routes Plum Blossom Broadsword, Liuhe Spear, Step Wonder Spear and Wensheng Sword. He is especially good at "scattered boxing" (Benquan Sanshou in Chinese Pinyin). On the basis of the original boxing skills, he is innovative. Song Lianhong expanded the elbow-type to attack the opponent's upper, middle and lower plates according to the movement characteristics, which enriched the application of traditional tactics in actual combats.

Song Lianhong has participated in many national, provincial and municipal martial arts competitions and won many awards. In 1986, Song Lianhong won the male lion prize in the National Martial Arts Observation and Exchange Conference. In 1988, Jining Martial Arts Sports Association recognized him as the municipal martial arts coach. In 2011, he won the gold medal in the National Meridian Gate Competition in Liangshan, Shandong Province. Over the years, Song Lianhong has taught more than 30 disciples, trained many fans of Wensheng Boxing, and has done a lot of work for the inheritance and development of Wensheng Boxing.

佛汉拳传承人——陈洪元

陈洪元，男，1951 年出生，山东东明人，佛汉拳第六代传承人。

佛汉拳，亦称“佛汉捶”，以掌法为主，朴实大方，注重实用，技击性强。据《佛汉拳谱》记载，佛汉出手站当阳，切闪调步人难防，两手不离胸，双肘不离肋，“身似弓，手似箭，鹰眼，猫腰，鬼拉转”，以擒拿对练、实战为主，辅以硬功。佛汉拳主要包括基本功(高低瞄)、佛汉散手单练套路、对练套路、擒拿硬功功法、拳理技法要求等五部分。佛汉拳融会了中国古典哲学、医学、武学、人体力学，遵循佛家、道家思想，特别是吸收了道家太极阴阳学论，刚柔相济，虚实分明，周身一家，浑圆一体，形成了独具特点的拳学体系。

陈洪元师从佛汉拳第五代传承人魏仁方、陈云汉、陈书贵，较系统、完整地继承了佛汉拳。他演练的佛汉拳套路大开大合，刚猛有力，气势磅礴，散手动作快如风、疾似雨，发力迅猛，他的铁爪功更是远近闻名。

多年来，陈洪元一直致力于佛汉拳的普及和推广，为佛汉拳传承事业做出了突出贡献。在闲暇之余，他和师弟不辞辛苦，亲自传授佛汉拳，几十年来培养了大批优秀的佛汉拳弟子，桃李满天下，深受人们敬重。其弟子分布山东、河南、浙江等 6 省 20 余县以及海外多国。七世弟子张少林参加在北京举办的“第二届亚太武术交流大会”并获得银牌奖，受到多名当代武学大师的称赞。

陈洪元现为东明县武术家协会副主席、东明县佛汉拳协会副主席，不断为佛汉拳的发展搭建更广阔的平台，在佛汉拳的传承中起到了承上启下的重要作用。

Chen Hongyuan—Inheritor of Fohan Boxing

Chen Hongyuan, male, born in Dongming County, Shandong Province in 1951, is the six-generation inheritor of Fohan Boxing.

Fohan Boxing, also known as "Fohan Pound", mainly adopting palm technique, is simple and generous, practical and skillful. According to the record of *Fohan Boxing Spectrum*, it is difficult to guard when Fohan starts to stand in *Dangyang*. His hands are not departing from his chest, his elbows are not departing from his ribs. "He is like a bow, his hands are like arrows, his eyes are like eagle's eyes, his waist is like cat's waist, and he is like a ghost pulling around." He mainly practices grasping and fighting, supplemented by solid work. The main contents of Fohan boxing include five parts. Following the thoughts of Buddhism and Taoism, Fohan Boxing integrates Chinese classical philosophy, medicine, martial arts and human mechanics. It absorbs the theory of *Tai Ji Yin Yang* of Taoism, which combines rigidity and softness, has clear virtual-real distinction, and forms an organic whole, hence a boxing system with unique characteristics.

Chen Hongyuan was apprenticed to the fifth generation inheritors of Fohan Boxing Wei Renfang, Chen Yunhan and Chen Shugui. His practice of Fohan Boxing routine is open and close, strong and powerful. His free-handed action is as fast as the wind and rain, and sends forth swiftly and violently. And his iron claw is well-known far and wide.

Over the years, Chen Hongyuan has been committed to the popularization and promotion of Fohan Boxing and has made outstanding contributions to its inheritance. In his spare time, he and his junior fellow apprentices spared no effort to teach Fohan Boxing in person. Over the past decades, he has trained a large number of excellent Fohan Boxing disciples. He has disciples all over the world and is highly respected by people. His disciples are distributed in more than 20 counties in six provinces, including Shandong, Henan and Zhejiang, as well as in many other countries. His disciple Zhang Shaolin of the seventh generation inheritors won the silver medal in the Second Asia-Pacific Martial Arts Exchange Conference held in Beijing and was praised by many contemporary martial arts masters.

Chen Hongyuan is the vice-chairman of Dongming Martial Arts Association and the vice-chairman of Dongming Fohan Boxing Association. He is devoted to building a broader platform for the development of Fohan Boxing and plays an important role in the inheritance of Fohan Boxing.

地龙经拳传承人——杜文明

杜文明，男，1956 年出生，山东高密人，地龙经拳第五代传承人。

地龙经拳因其套路动作多以腾空跳跃、跌扑翻滚为主而得名,人称“腰身柔灵翻滚巧，随势跌扑似虎豹”。地龙经拳有完整的拳法体系，主要拳法分前后左右、高低远近、伸缩弯曲、翻转腾挪等路数。套路有上盘套路和下盘套路两部：上盘套路有鸳鸯脚拳架、六和拳、次六和拳等；下盘套路有骨寸腿拳架、中风剪拳架等。主要腿法有剪蹬、蹦、缠、绞、绊、踩等。地龙经拳的每个拳法和套路都有具体要求，饱含浓郁的地方特色。

杜文明自 13 岁开始习练高密地龙经拳，拜地龙经拳第四代传承人官星南为师。他不畏艰苦,从基本功（跨虎步）开始练习地龙经拳。凭借着对地龙经拳的热爱和老师的精心栽培，杜文明深得地龙经拳精髓，并谨遵老师嘱托，努力传承和发展地龙经拳。

熟练掌握地龙经拳套路后，在其内容、动作不变的情况下，杜文明使每一个套路都具有可以领拳（领方甘当“活靶子，捶垫子”配合对方，给对方“喂招”）的特征。他的招式主要以倒地为主，远距离发力攻击对方，如腰部以下攻击反关节，而且有很多败中取胜的动作，如大挑、朝天脚、倒、天罗网等。再如用腿攻击对方，两腿打人，体现出地龙经拳蹿、蹦、跳、跃身轻如燕的特点。

2010 年 8 月，杜文明成为山东省传统武术项目一级裁判员，同年 12 月由中国武术协会吸收为中国武术协会会员。杜文明常年坚持开展传习活动，与其子弟积极参加政府组织的非物质文化遗产保护宣传和展演活动。在杜文明的悉心教导下，弟子们刻苦努力，经常参加全国各地举行的武术比赛，不断刷新战绩。

Du Wenming—Inheritor of Dilongjing Boxing

Du Wenming, male, born in Gaomi, Shandong Province in 1956, is the fifth-generation inheritor of Dilongjing Boxing.

Dilongjing Boxing is named for its routine movements, which mainly include leaping in the air, tumbling and rolling. Dilongjing Boxing has a complete system of boxing techniques, of which the dominant are the front and back, left and right, high and low, far and near, flexion and bending, turning and moving. There are two sets of routes: upper and lower. The main leg techniques are scissors, jumps, entanglements, twists, trips, tramples and so on. Every technique and routine of Dilongjing Boxing should meet specific requirements, and is full of strong local characteristics.

Du Wenming began to practice Gaomi Dilongjing Boxing at the age of 13, and he took the fourth generation inheritor of Dilongjing Boxing Guan Xingnan as the teacher. He did not fear hardships and began to practice Dilongjing Boxing from the basic skill (cross tiger step). With his love for Dilongjing Boxing and the careful cultivation of his teachers, Du Wenming has acquired the essence of Dilongjing Boxing, and he has made great efforts to inherit and develop the Dilongjing Boxing in accordance with the instructions of his teachers.

After mastering the Dilongjing Boxing routes skillfully, Du Wenming makes every route characterized by being capable of leading the fist (the leader is willing to be a "live target or thump mat" to cooperate with and feed the other side) under the condition that its content and action remain unchanged. His tactics are mainly to fall to the ground and to attack the other side from a long distance.

In August 2010, Du Wenming became the first-level referee of traditional martial arts events in Shandong Province. In December of the same year, Du Wenming was absorbed by the Chinese Martial Arts Association as a member. Du Wenming persisted in carrying out the activities of inheritance all the year round, and actively participated in the propaganda and exhibition activities of intangible cultural heritage protection organized by the government with his children. Under the careful instruction of Du Wenming, his disciples worked hard and often participated in martial arts competitions held throughout the country and constantly refresh the achievements.

武当太乙门传承人——林树基

林树基，男，1950 年出生，山东济南人，中国武术协会会员，武当太乙门第四代传承人。

武当太乙门主要内容有十二路弹腿、太乙埋伏拳、太乙金刚拳、太乙玄门剑、太乙缠丝刀、太乙五虎枪、太乙徒手对练、养生功法等。济南武当太乙门的优秀代表套路是醉拳和猴拳。醉拳善醉步，在醉意及踉跄步中，寻找攻防时机，趁人不备伺机出击。猴拳具猴之灵性，动作机敏、轻灵。武当太乙门将“道”的舒缓，与其他拳种刚健有力、朴实无华的特点有机地结合，既具有重技击、重形象等特点，又具有“道拳一体”“内外合一”“柔中寓刚”“刚柔相济”“动静相生”的特点，实现了“性命双修”的主旨。

林树基自幼跟随父亲林信斋（武当太乙门第三代传承人）习练太乙门派各项拳、械以及散手等项目，潜心整理拳理，同时协助父亲义务授徒，经常参加相关部门组织的义务慰问演出。

潜心习武之余，林树基还特别注重武当太乙门的发展传承。他于 2011 年开始进入学校推广太乙门武术，弘扬中华传统武术精神，激发青少年热爱传统武术的习武热情。近年来，林树基带领学生积极参加公益表演、“非遗”展示及武术比赛等各项活动，2008 年以来他所教授的学生有 100 余人参加了全国、省、市各级武术比赛，获得金、银、铜牌总计 200 余枚。林树基个人成绩显著，2009 年，他参加了在梁山举办的第八届“全国子午门少林民间武术争霸赛”，演练武当太乙拳，获得金牌。

Lin Shuji—Inheritor of Wudang Taiyimen

Lin Shuji, male, born in Jinan, Shandong Province in 1950, is a member of China Martial Arts Association and the fourth generation inheritor of Wudang Taiyimen.

The main contents of Wudang Taiyimen include twelve routes of martial arts, taiyi ambush boxing, taiyi jingang boxing, taiyi xuanmen sword, taiyi winding screwdriver, taiyi five-tiger spear, taiyi bare-handed pair training, health preservation skills, and etc. Jinan Wudang Taiyimen excellent representative routes are Drunk Boxing and Monkey Boxing. Drunk Boxing is good at drunk steps, looking for attack and defense opportunities in drunk and staggering steps, taking advantage of people's unprepared state to attack. Monkey boxing has the intelligence of monkeys, quick and light in action. Wudang Taiyimen organically combined the relaxation of Tao with the strong, simple and unadorned characteristics of other kinds of boxing. It highlights tactic attack and the image. It is characterized by "the integration of Tao and Boxing" "the integration of inside and outside" "the combination of flexiblility and rigidity" "the combination of hardness and softness" and "the combination of movement and quietness". It achieves the goal of "double cultivation of character and destiny".

Lin Shuji followed his father Lin Xinzhai (the third generation inheritor of Wudang Taiyimen) since his childhood to practice the various boxings, weapons and karates of Taiyimen, and devoted himself to sorting out boxing principles. At the same time, he assisted his father in voluntary teaching and often participated in voluntary consolation performances organized by relevant departments.

In addition to practicing martial arts, Lin Shuji also pays special attention to the development and inheritance of Wudang Taiyimen. In 2011, he began to promote Taiyimen martial arts in schools, and stimulate young people's enthusiasm for traditional martial arts. In recent years, Lin Shuji has led students to actively participate in public welfare performances, intangible cultural heritage exhibitions and martial arts competitions. Since 2008, more than 100 of his students have participated in national, provincial and municipal martial arts competitions, and won more than 200 gold, silver and bronze medals. Lin Shuji has made remarkable personal achievements. In 2009, he participated in the National Meridian Gate Shaolin Folk Martial Arts Competition held in Liangshan, where he practiced Wudang Taiyimen Boxing and won the gold medal.

傳承人

传统美术

Traditional Arts

东昌葫芦雕刻传承人——王树峰

王树峰，男，1983年出生，山东聊城人，东昌葫芦雕刻第六代传承人，山东省农村优秀文化人才。

东昌葫芦雕刻起源于宋代，当时宫廷艺人王合尚在葫芦上雕刻出精美图案用来养蝈蝈，当地人纷纷效仿，东昌葫芦雕刻便逐渐流传开来。东昌葫芦雕刻用料考究，刻工纯熟，图案丰富，制作精良。其用料多以大葫芦、亚腰葫芦和扁圆葫芦为主，雕刻借鉴镂雕技法，将构图以外的空白部分全部镂空，透刻上折线纹、如意纹、古钱纹等各式花纹。题材内容多以写实性的花鸟、鱼虫、走兽、人物、山水居多，其中人物雕刻的取材尤为丰富。东昌葫芦雕刻艺术风格淳朴、典雅，洋溢着浓郁的乡土气息。

王树峰学生时期喜爱绘画，主攻山水花鸟画，为学习东昌葫芦雕刻奠定了基础。自2003年开始，王树峰一直致力于对东昌葫芦雕刻技艺的研究与实践。他先是受教于聊城市工艺美术技师郎树山，2011年拜东昌葫芦雕刻国家级传承人李玉成为师，成为东昌葫芦雕刻第六代传承人，深得东昌葫芦雕刻闫寺流派“以线为本，三土一老”特色的精髓。

王树峰的葫芦雕刻充分保持了东昌葫芦雕刻技艺的本真性、完整性和核心技艺的唯一性，所刻作品形神兼备。他在精心钻研继承传统雕刻技艺的同时兼借烙绘之法，把中国水墨、线画的风格融进东昌葫芦雕刻中，开创了东昌葫芦的新路新风。王树峰综合能力强，将雕、刻、烙、研、染、托、衬等数技并兼运用于创作，为东昌葫芦雕刻开辟更加广阔的发展空间。

王树峰技艺精湛，先后获得过多项大奖，其葫芦雕刻及烙烩等作品受到专家好评，并被社会各界人士收藏。此外，为把东昌葫芦雕刻进一步发扬光大，王树峰在师傅的支持下，自2012年开始授徒，入门徒弟舒宏力现已能独立操刀入行，并已在东昌葫芦工艺界小有名气。

Wang Shufeng—
Inheritor of Dongchang Gourd Sculpture

Wang Shufeng, male, born in Liaocheng, Shandong Province in 1983, is the sixth generation inheritor of Dongchang Gourd Sculpture. He is an excellent cultural talent in rural areas of Shandong Province.

Dongchang Gourd Sculpture originated in the Song Dynasty. At that time, Wang Heshang, a court artist, carved exquisite patterns on the gourd to raise scorpions. The locals followed suit, and Dongchang Gourd Sculpture gradually spread. Dongchang gourd sculpture requires fastidious materials, skilled carver, rich patterns, and excellent production. Its materials mainly include big gourd, sub-waist gourd and flat round gourd. Using engraving techniques for reference, the blank parts outside the composition are hollowed out, and various patterns such as folded lines, idealistic lines and ancient money lines are carved. Most of the subjects are realistic flowers and birds, fish and insects, animals, characters, mountains and rivers, among which the material of character sculpture is particularly rich. The style of Dongchang gourd sculpture is simple, elegant, and full of strong local flavor.

Wang Shufeng loved painting in his school days, and mainly focused on landscape, flower and bird painting, which laid a foundation for learning Dongchang Gourd Sculpture later. Since 2003, Wang Shufeng has been devoting himself to the research and practice of Dongchang Gourd Sculpture. He was first taught by Liaocheng craft and art technician Lang Shushan. In 2011, he was apprenticed to Li Yu, the national inheritor of Dongchang Gourd Sculpture, and became the sixth generation inheritor of Dongchang Gourd Sculpture. He gained the essence of "draft-based, three-earthy-one-old" Yansi genre of Dongchang Gourd Sculpture.

Wang Shufeng's gourd sculpture fully maintains the authenticity, integrity and uniqueness of the core skills of Dongchang Gourd Sculpture, and his works are vivid both physically and spiritually. While carefully studying and inheriting the traditional sculpture skills, he also used the method of branding to integrate the Chinese ink and line painting style into Dongchang gourd sculpture, creating a new way and new style of Dongchang gourd. Wang Shufeng has strong comprehensive ability. He combines sculpture, engraving, brazing, polishing, dyeing, supporting and lining and other techniques to create a broader space for the development of Dongchang Gourd Sculpture.

Wang Shufeng has won many awards for his exquisite skills. His gourd sculptures and branding works are well received by experts and collected by people from all walks of life. In addition, in order to further develop Dongchang gourd sculpture, Wang Shufeng, with the support of his teachers, began to teach apprentices in 2012. Shu Hongli, an admitted apprentice, has been able to work independently and has a certain reputation in Dongchang Gourd Sculpture craft circle.

曹州面人传承人——李双虎

李双虎，男，1966年出生，山东菏泽马岭岗镇桥李村人。

菏泽古称“曹州”，曹州面人是古曹州三绝之一，距今已有近2000年的历史。其造型概括，简练生动，形象传神，比例夸张适当，色彩艳丽单纯，与中国的大写意国画艺术有异曲同工之妙。

李双虎出生于面塑世家，是面塑大师李芳清的关门弟子。他从6岁开始学习面塑，至今已有40余年。几十年的学习和实践，让李双虎成长为一名出色的面塑艺人。自20世纪80年代以来，李双虎经常在公共场馆献艺交流。2002年，李双虎应邀参加第三届山东省民间艺术节。2003年，李双虎和师傅李芳清一起为山东电视台齐鲁民俗节目组做专题介绍《齐鲁民俗——菏泽面塑》。

李双虎在秉承传统的基础上推陈出新，使传统艺术与现代艺术恰到好处地融为一体。他的面塑作品形式多样、取材广泛，有鲁西南花供，人物造像、花鸟鱼虫、瓜果蔬菜和牛肉排骨等红白案之类上百种，造型简练，精美细腻，惟妙惟肖。

凭借精湛的技艺，李双虎多次参加比赛并获奖。2008年，其面塑作品在“黄河口杯”2009山东省旅游商品展暨“好客山东”游客最喜爱的山东省标志性旅游商品评选中荣获银奖。2009年，作品《关公》在第二届山东国际大众艺术节——2009齐鲁民间艺术博览交易会评奖中获得银奖。2012年，作品《四大天王》在第二届中国菏泽艺术节获得金草根奖。2013年，代表作《关公》《莲生贵子》《穆桂英》《平安春信》等被选入《中国民间文艺家大辞典》。与此同时，李双虎还积极致力于面塑传承工作，教授过的徒弟有姚军、张夕晨、陈付生等。

Li Shuanghu—Inheritor of Caozhou Dough Modeling

Li Shuanghu, male, born in 1966, is a native of Qiaoli Village, Malinggang Town, Heze, Shandong Province.

Heze was called "Caozhou" in ancient times. Caozhou dough modeling was one of the three greatest wonders in ancient Caozhou. It has a history of nearly 2000 years. Its modeling was concise, succinct and lively, expressive and vivid. The proportion was exaggerated appropriately, and the color was gorgeous and simple, which was similar to Chinese freehand brushwork art.

Li Shuanghu was born in a family of dough modeling. He was a disciple of Li Fangqing, a master of dough modeling. He began to study dough modeling at the age of 6, and has been studying it for more than 40 years. After decades of study and practice, Li Shuanghu has grown into an outstanding dough modeling artist. Since the 1980s, Li Shuanghu has often performanced in public venues. In 2002, he was invited to participate in the third Shandong Folk Art Festival. In 2003, Li Shuanghu and his master Li Fangqing jointly made a special column "Qilu Folklore—Heze Dough Modeling" for Qilu Folklore Program of Shandong TV Station.

Li Shuanghu, adhering to the tradition, pushes forward the old and brings forth the new, which makes the traditional art and the modern art merge properly. His dough modeling sculptures are in various forms and adopt wide materials, including hundreds of red and white materials such as flowers in southwest Shandong, characters, flowers, birds, fish and insects, melons, fruits, vegetables and beef ribs, etc. They are concise, exquisite and lifelike.

With exquisite skills, Li Shuanghu has participated in many competitions and won prizes. In 2008, his dough modeling sculptures won the silver prize in the "Yellow River Estuary Cup" Shandong Tourism Commodity Exhibition in 2009, namely the "Hospitality Shandong" tourists' favorite landmark tourism commodity selection of Shandong Province. In 2009, his masterpiece *Guan Gong* won the silver prize in the second Shandong International Popular Arts Festival—2009 Qilu Folk Art Fair. In 2012, his work *Four Heavenly Kings* won the golden grass root award at the second Heze Art Festival of China. In 2013, his representative works *Guan Gong, Lotus Gave Birth to a Noble Son*, *Mu Guiying* and *The Spring Letter of Safety* were selected into the *Great Dictionary of Chinese Folk Writers and Artists*. At the same time, Li Shuanghu is actively committed to the inheritance of dough modeling. His disciples include Yao Jun, Zhang Xichen and Chen Fusheng, etc.

聂家庄泥塑传承人——聂臣希

聂臣希，男，1965年出生，山东高密姜庄镇聂家庄西村人。

聂家庄泥塑是高密民间艺术“三绝”之一，起源于明万历年间，迄今已有400余年的历史。其题材范围有历史传说、神话故事、花鸟鱼虫等。艺术造型古朴夸张，粗犷豪放，构图完整，注重写意。用色少而精，以桃红和大绿为主衬托动物和人的神情，在全国泥塑中别具一格。能动能响的巧妙设计，更是聂家庄泥塑区别于其他泥塑的最大特征。

聂臣希的父母都是泥塑制作艺人，受家庭熏陶，他从小热爱泥塑，10岁就能制作简单的泥塑作品。随着技艺的提高，聂臣希开始和父母一起制作复杂的泥塑产品。改革开放后，随着国家对民间艺术的重视，聂臣希扩大规模，成立了聂鹏泥塑作坊，并组织了一些有经验的艺人从事泥塑的初期制作工序，更好地传承民间泥塑制作艺术。

聂臣希的泥塑作品造型优美，大胆夸张，色彩光鲜艳丽，对比鲜明，借鉴扑灰年画的绘画技艺，突出大红大绿，用黑色提神、紫色点缀，鲜艳明目而又柔和动人。他在继承传统的基础上认真钻研，设计制作了摇动能响的《母子猴》和《吧嗒孩》等新作品。同时，他通过实践，解决了聂家庄泥塑生产受季节影响等问题。

聂臣希经常参加文化艺术和展演活动，通过活动让更多人认识了聂家庄泥塑。2010年，其作品《叫虎》《抱鱼娃》等进入中国上海世博会。2011年，赴台湾和澳门进行非物质文化遗产展演。2012年，参加第二届中国非物质文化遗产博览会，并获得传承人展示奖。2013年，聂家庄泥塑在CCTV–4《走遍中国》栏目中被介绍展示。同年，在山东省民俗文化博览会中，泥塑《叫虎》系列被山东省民间文艺家协会评为金奖。

为更好地传承聂家庄泥塑，聂臣希不但将泥塑技艺传给了儿子聂鹏，还经常到中小学校义务传授泥塑制作技艺，并与天津科技大学协商成立了大学生社会实践基地，让更多学生感受聂家庄泥塑的魅力。

Nie Chenxi—Inheritor of Niejiazhuang Clay Sculpture

Nie Chenxi, male, born in 1965, is from Nie Jiazhuang West Village, Jiangzhuang Town, Gaomi, Shandong Province.

Niejiazhuang Clay Sculpture is one of the "three wonders" of Gaomi folk art, which originated in the Ming Dynasty and has a history of more than 400 years. Its themes range from historical legends, myths and stories to flowers, birds, fish and insects. The artistic form is simple and exaggerated, rough and bold, complete in composition, and emphasizes the expression of the spirit. The number of color is few but exact, with peach red and big green as the main colors to foil the animal and human expression, which is unique in the clay sculpture nationwide. The ingenious design of dynamic energy is the most distinguishing feature of Niejiazhuang Clay Sculpture.

Nie Chenxi's parents are clay sculpture artists. Influenced by his family, Nie Chenxi was fond of clay sculpture when he was young and could make simple clay sculptures at the age of 10. With the improvement of skills, Nie Chenxi began to make complex clay products with his parents. After the reform and opening up, Nie Chenxi expanded the scale, established Nie Peng clay sculpture workshop, and organized some experienced artists to engage in the initial production process of clay sculpture, so as to better inherit the production art of folk clay sculpture.

Nie Chenxi's clay sculptures are beautiful and bold. The colors are bright and contrasting. Drawing on the experience of the painting skills of the Puhui New Year Painting, his works highlight the bright red and green, with black and purple as foils. On the basis of inheriting the tradition, he designed some new works such as *Mother and Baby Monkeys* and *Babbling Kids*. Meanwhile, he solved the seasonally dependent problem of Niejiazhuang Clay Sculpture Production through practice.

Nie Chenxi often participates in arts and cultural activities, which makes Nie Jiazhuang Clay Sculpture more widely known. In 2010, his works *Tiger* and *Fish Baby* were exhibited on Shanghai World Expo. In 2011, he went to Taiwan and Macao for intangible cultural heritage exhibitions. In 2012, he participated in the second China Intangible Cultural Heritage Exposition and won the exhibition prize for inheritors. In 2013, Niejiazhuang Clay Sculpture was introduced by the *Travel Through China* column on CCTV-4. In the same year, in Shandong Folk Culture Expo, his clay sculpture *Tiger* series were awarded the gold medal by Shandong Folk Literature and Art Association.

In order to better inherit Nie Jiazhuang Clay Sculpture, Nie Chenxi not only passed on the clay sculpture skills to his son Nie Peng, but also taught the production techniques of clay sculpture in primary and secondary schools. He also established a social practice base for college students in consultation with Tianjin University of Science and Technology, so that more students can feel the charm of Nie Jiazhuang Clay Sculpture.

苍山泥塑传承人——刘福祥

刘福祥，男，1944年出生，山东临沂人，苍山泥塑第五代传承人。

泥塑就是我们平常所说的“捏泥人”。苍山泥塑起源于清咸丰年间，至今已有100余年的历史。其题材广泛，既有人物、神像，又有飞禽走兽、果蔬食品，种类多样。苍山泥塑造型完整统一，夸张而又逼真，简洁而不粗俗，富有浓郁的乡土气息，被社会各界称为“小郭泥塑”。

刘福祥自幼便跟随父亲学习泥塑玩具制作，1963年初中毕业后在家务农，利用农闲时节捏制泥塑作品出售补贴家用，经过50多年的沉淀，刘福祥已系统地掌握了泥塑制作工艺，创作了一批适应新形势的泥塑作品，以其质朴无华、平凡自然的艺术魅力，倍受老百姓喜爱。

苍山泥塑采取精工细作的制作方法，工序多达30多道，刘福祥在继承传统制作技艺的基础上，将泥塑作品与现代戏剧、年画、工艺美术进行了结合，善于抓住戏曲中最具代表性的情节和人物特征进行创作，能巧妙地压缩人体比例，简略人体四肢，给泥人以横向的夸张，从而达到“不似之似”的效果。同时，刘福祥创作的泥塑作品色彩鲜明，装饰味浓，色彩运用以白、红、绿、黄、黑为主，用色简洁明快，体现了鲜明的地域特色。

刘福祥多年来一直致力于苍山泥塑的创作、传承与保护，积极培养泥塑传承人，将这一传统工艺传承下去，同时获得多个奖项。2003年，在临沂市首届民间艺术展览中，其创作的泥塑作品荣获一等奖。2009年，其作品《鱼头娃》《三国戏曲人物》等9件作品被无锡中国泥人博物馆收藏。因表现突出，刘福祥于2010年成为中国民间工艺美术协会会员。

Liu Fuxiang—Inheritor of Cangshan Clay Sculpture

Liu Fuxiang, male, born in 1944, is a native of Linyi City, Shandong Province and the fifth generation inheritor of Cangshan Clay Sculpture.

The clay sculpture is often called "clay figurine". Cangshan Clay Sculpture originated in the Xianfeng Reign of the Qing Dynasty, which has a history of more than 100 years. It has a wide range of subjects, including characters, gods, birds, animals, fruits, vegetables and food, etc. Cangshan Clay Sculpture is complete and unified, exaggerated and realistic, concise but not vulgar, rich in local flavor, and is also known as "Xiaoguo clay sculpture" by all walks of life.

Liu Fuxiang learned clay sculpture toy making from his father in his childhood. After graduating from junior high school in 1963, he made a living by farming and sold clay sculpture works to subsidize his family during the slack season in farming. After more than 50 years of precipitation, Liu Fuxiang has systematically mastered the clay sculpture making process and created a number of clay sculpture works adapted to the new situation. With their simple, ordinary and natural artistic charm, Liu Fuxiang's works have been popular with by the people.

Cangshan Clay Sculpture adopts elaborate production techniques with over 30 working procedures. On the basis of inheriting traditional production techniques, Liu Fuxiang combines clay sculptures with modern dramas, new year pictures and industrial art. He is good at grasping the most representative plots and characters in operas to create clay sculptures, so as to achieve the "between unlike and like" effect. At the same time, Liu Fuxiang's clay sculpture works have bright colors and strong decorative flavor. The main colors are white, red, green, yellow and black. The color choice is concise and lively, which reflects the distinct regional characteristics.

Liu Fuxiang has been dedicated to the creation, inheritance and protection of Cangshan Clay Sculpture for many years. He has actively trained the inheritors of clay sculpture, passed on this traditional craft and won many awards at the same time. In 2003, his clay sculptures won the first prize on the first Folk Art Exhibition of Linyi. In 2009, nine of his works, such as *Fish Head Doll* and *Three Kingdoms Opera Figures*, were collected by Wuxi Museum of Chinese Clay Sculpture. Because of his outstanding achievements, Liu Fuxiang became a member of China Folk Arts and Crafts Association in 2010.

高密剪纸传承人——曹兆爱

曹兆爱，女，1955 年出生，山东高密人，高密剪纸第四代传承人。

高密剪纸是山东省高密市民间艺术“三绝”之一，以内涵丰富和技艺精湛闻名于世。高密剪纸题材范围广泛，传说、神话、故事、戏剧人物、花鸟草虫无所不包。在形象刻画上，注重夸张而不失真；在艺术风格上，讲究阴剪与阳剪手法并用，巧用黑块和细线，善使锯齿纹和光滑面，制作出的剪纸简约而不单调，生动而又传神。

曹兆爱自幼便表现出对剪纸的兴趣，10 岁时，母亲便开始教曹兆爱学习剪纸。1974 年参加工作后，曹兆爱利用业余时间进行剪纸艺术的创作。2009 年 3 月，成为中国传媒大学影视艺术学院（民间文化创研基地）特聘研究员，开始专业从事剪纸艺术的创作和教学。

在继承传统技艺的基础上，曹兆爱在剪纸内容上进行了创新，形成了自己独特的风格：在色彩上，善于用大红色单色剪纸。在线条上，继承了外祖母和母亲在剪纸线条上的纤细优美和精巧。在内容上，将传统美与现代美进行结合，把古代的“老花样”运用到反映现代生活的作品中，古今相糅，既有传统的表现手法，又打破了单调的古老表现主题；在风格上，将剪纸艺术和书法艺术相结合，使剪纸作品独树一帜，具有更加浓厚的文化底蕴。

受曹兆爱的影响，其外甥女岳颖和刘卫卫、学生王鹤也跟其学习剪纸，现在三人已能独立创作一些作品，并能熟练地剪出上百种传统图案。曹兆爱的剪纸作品也获得了社会的认可，多项作品获国家及省、市级奖项，并被博物馆收藏展览。2008 年 4 月《环球人物》以《放不下的“金剪子”》为题对其进行了报道。曹兆爱在保护高密剪纸的路上不断前进，为高密剪纸的传承做出了重要贡献。

Cao Zhao'ai— Inheritor of Gaomi Paper Cutting

Cao Zhao'ai, female, born in 1955, Gaomi, Shandong Province, is the fourth generation inheritor of Gaomi Paper Cutting.

Gaomi Paper Cutting is one of the three wonders of Gaomi folk art in Shandong Province. It is famous for its rich connotation and exquisite skills. Gaomi Paper Cutting has a wide range of subjects, including legends, myths, stories, dramatic characters, flowers, birds, grass and insects, etc. as far as the image depiction is concerned, emphasis is laid on exaggeration without distortion; as far as the artistic style is concerned, emphasis is laid on the combination of Yin-shear and Yang-shear techniques. It skillfully uses black blocks and fine lines, and is good at making serrated lines and smooth surfaces. The Gaomi Paper Cutting works are simple but not monotonous, vivid and lifelike.

Cao Zhao'ai showed an interest in paper cutting at an early age. When she was 10 years old, her mother began to teach her paper cutting. After starting work in 1974, Cao Zhao'ai used her spare time to create paper cutting works. In March 2009, she became a special researcher in the Founding Research Base of Folk Culture of the School of Film and Television Arts of China Media University, and began to specialize in the creation and teaching of paper cutting art.

On the basis of inheriting traditional skills, Cao Zhao'ai innovates the themes of paper cutting and formed her own unique style. In terms of color, Cao Zhao'ai is good at using bright red. In terms of line, she inherits the fine gracefulness and delicacy of her grandmother and mother. In terms of themes, she combines traditional beauty with modern beauty, combines ancient and modern methods of expression, and breaks the monotonous theme of ancient expression. In terms of style, her paper cutting works have more cultural connotation by combining paper cutting art with calligraphy art.

Under Cao Zhao'ai's influence, her nieces Yue Ying and Liu Weiwei and her student Wang He started to learn paper cutting from her. Now each of them has been able to create some works independently and skillfully cut out hundreds of traditional patterns. Cao Zhao'ai's paper cutting works have also been recognized by society, and many of them have won national and provincial and municipal awards and have been exhibited in museums. In April 2008, Cao Zhao'ai's story was reported by *Global Characters* under the title of *Inseparable Golden Scissors*. Cao Zhao'ai has made great contributions to the inheritance and dissemination of Gaomi Paper Cutting.

烟台剪纸传承人——栾淑娟

栾淑娟，女，1956 年出生，山东烟台人，山东省民间手工艺制作大师，山东省传统技艺大师。

剪纸在烟台一带流行，始于明朝。其形式多样，包括单色剪纸、勾绘染色剪纸、拼色剪纸和衬色剪纸。传统的烟台剪纸多用红色，色红而不艳，悦目耐看。在整体风格上，烟台剪纸表现出画风紧凑、线条挺拔流畅的特点，既具有朴素性、广泛性、随意性、谐音双关等特性，也具有重要的历史价值和实用价值。

在家庭的影响下，栾淑娟自幼酷爱剪纸艺术，10 岁时便跟随祖母学习剪纸，悟性极高，很快在乡里便小有名气，逢节赶集用剪纸收入贴补家用。1971 年从学校毕业后，栾淑娟就一直从事剪纸研究、创作和传承，获得了一系列荣誉。现在，栾淑娟的剪纸作品已被美国、德国等国外人士求购和收藏。

栾淑娟继承和发展了烟台剪纸“细”和“活”的特色，花虫鱼鸟、十二生肖、卡通人物等信手拈来，作品惟妙惟肖，细腻精巧，极具民间特色。凭借多年经验，栾淑娟形成了自己独特的剪纸风格，在剪纸过程中善于任意取舍、大胆创造，在保留传统写实风格的基础上，又将现实以艺术的形式再现，制作出的作品玲珑剔透、雅俗共赏，深受老百姓的喜爱。

在栾淑娟的努力下，来自全国各地 70 多位传承人跟随其学习。栾淑娟的作品也得到了社会的认可，获得了多项国家及省、市级奖项。2008 年，作品《平安奥运》在全国剪纸大赛中获金奖；2010 年，作品《百子寿》在第五届中国文艺博览会上获金奖；2012 年 8 月，作品《龙凤呈祥》在全国第四届文博会上获金奖。因表现突出，2011 年栾淑娟被山东省文化厅授予“山东省农村优秀文化人才”称号。

Luan Shujuan—Inheritor of Yantai Paper Cutting

Luan Shujuan, female, born in 1956, is from Yantai, Shandong Province. She is a master of folk crafts and a master of traditional skills in Shandong Province.

Paper cutting is popular in Yantai area, which began in the Ming Dynasty at the latest. Its forms are varied, including monochrome paper cutting, sketch-dyed paper cutting, color-matched paper cutting and color-lined paper cutting. Traditional Yantai paper cutting is mostly red, which is gorgeous, pleasant and durable. As to the overall style, it shows the characteristics of compact style and smooth lines. It is characterized by its simplicity, universality, randomness, homophonic pun, and has significant historical and practical value.

Under the influence of the family, Luan Shujuan has been greatly fond of the art of paper cutting since her childhood. When she was 10 years old, she followed her grandmother to learn paper cutting. She was very savvy and soon became famous in the countryside. After graduating from school in 1971, Luan Shujuan has been engaged in paper cutting research, creation and inheritance, and has won a series of honors. Now, Luan Shujuan's paper cutting works have been sought and collected by foreign people from countries such as the United States and Germany.

Luan Shujuan inherits and develops the "fine" and "agile" features of Yantai Paper Cutting with flowers, insects, fish and birds, zodiac, and cartoon characters, etc. The works are vivid, delicate and exquisite, with abundant folk characteristics. With many years of experience, Luan Shujuan has formed her own unique paper cutting style. She tends to make arbitrary choices and creates boldly in the process of paper cutting. On the basis of retaining the traditional realistic style, she reproduces the reality in the form of art. The works she produces are exquisitely carved, and are much appreciated by the people from all walks of life.

With Luan Shujuan's efforts, more than 70 inheritors from all over the country followed her to learn paper cutting. Luan Shujuan's works have also been recognized by the society and have won a number of national and provincial and municipal awards. In 2008, her work *Peaceful Olympics* won the gold medal in the national paper cutting competition; in 2010, *Baizishou* won the gold medal in the Fifth Chinese Art Exposition; and in August 2012, *The Dragon and Phoenix Bring Out Prosperity* won the gold medal in the Fourth National Cultural Exposition. Because of her outstanding achievements, she was awarded the title of "Excellent Cultural Talents in Rural Areas of Shandong Province" by Shandong Provincial Department of Culture and Tourism in 2011.

济宁面塑传承人——李刚

李刚，男，1968年出生，山东济宁人，济宁“十大民间手工艺人”。

济宁面塑是用糯米粉和面加彩后，用剪刀、拨子、刀子、梳子、镊子、铜丝等自制工具，通过压、按、点等手法塑造出各种动物、植物、人物造型的传统技艺。其色彩鲜明，色调明确，生动传神，栩栩如生，具有中国传统绘画的风采和神韵，又不失民间艺术的淳朴气息。如今的济宁面塑，有的可供使用，有的则因其较高的艺术价值而成为收藏品。

李刚自幼喜爱面塑制作，11岁便拜新新糕点厂高满囤为师。高满囤师承著名“万成公”糕点技师高福堂，善作贡品，在当地颇有影响，所做花贡以品种繁多、形象逼真、端庄素雅著称。济宁因水而生，有祭河神习俗，登门求高满囤做贡品者络绎不绝。李刚自小耳濡目染，后跟随高满囤学习并创新，形成了独特的李氏风格。

在老师高满囤的悉心传授下，李刚继承了传统济宁面塑制作技艺，并形成了自己独特的风格。在作品中融入书法观念，寓动于静，通过曲与直、直与折等对比，表现人物的灵动；同时注重人物外露部分，结合写意、夸张、工笔之法，面部注重五官，五官注重眼睛。色彩上也进行了创新，在继承传统面塑大红大绿对比色的基础上，借鉴国画调色之法，增加了过渡色。人物服饰上也有突破，坚持服饰服务人物“神”的展现，通过线、面、点以及小饰品的点缀，增强立体效果。在创作过程中，李刚总结经验并创立揉、捏、揪、挑、压、搓、滚、碾、剁、拨、按、切等“李氏十二法”，使人物刻画更加细腻，也更有利于后代学习与传承。

李刚先后举办面塑培训班20余期，培训学生近100人，与市教育局联合开展面塑进课堂活动160多人次，促进了济宁面塑的传播与传承。

Li Gang—Inheritor of Jining Dough Modeling

Li Gang, male, born in 1968, is a native of Jining, Shandong Province. He is one of the "Top Ten Folk Craftsmen" in Jining.

Jining Dough Modeling is a traditional technique of molding animals, plants and characters by pushing, pressing and dotting with self-made tools such as scissors, pokers, knives, combs, tweezers and copper wires with glutinous rice flour and colored dough. With bright colors and clear tone, it is vivid and lifelike, blending the style and charm of traditional Chinese painting and the simple flavor of folk art. Nowadays, some Jining Dough Sculptures are available for practical use, while others have become collections because of their high artistic values.

Li Gang has been fond of making dough sculptures since his childhood. When he was 11 years old, he took Gao Mantun from Xinxin Pastry Factory as his teacher. By being apprenticed to a famous pastry technician Gao Futang, Gao Mantun became good at making worship food and had a considerable influence in the local area. He is famous for his variety, vivid image and elegance. Jining came into being because the river, and there is a custom of offering sacrifices to river gods. There are a lot of people who go to visit Gao Mantun to seek his dough sculptures to worship gods. Being influenced from his childhood and following Gao Mantun to learn and innovate, Li Gang formed a unique "Li" style.

Under the careful instruction of Gao Mantun, Li Gang inherited the traditional techniques of Jining Dough Modeling and formed his own unique style. The works are injected the concept of calligraphy, showing motion through calmness and expressing people's agility through the comparison of curves and lines, lines and folds. Meanwhile, the works highlight the outward appearance of the characters, combining freehand brushwork, exaggeration and meticulous brushwork, paying attention to facial features and eyes. Innovations have also been made in color. On the basis of the contrast of red and green in traditional facial sculpture, transitional colors have been added by drawing with the techniques of color matching in traditional Chinese paintings. On the basis of traditional craftsmanship, breakthroughs have also been made in costumes. It is believed that the costumes serve the presentation of the characters' spirit, enhancing the three-dimensional effect through the embellishment of lines, surfaces, dots and small ornaments. In the process of creation, Li Gang summed up his experience and created Li's twelve methods of kneading, crumbing, pinching, tugging, pressing, rubbing, rolling, twisting, chopping, fiddling, holding, and cutting, which make the characterization more delicate and easy for future generations to learn and inherit.

Li Gang has held more than 20 training courses on dough modeling, taught nearly 100 students, and jointly carried out more than 160 classroom activities with the Jining Municipal Bureau of Education, which has promoted the spread and inheritance of Jining Dough Modeling.

济南面塑传承人——董凤岐

董凤岐，女，1939年出生，北京人，山东省工艺美术大师，山东省传统技艺大师。

济南面塑是以面粉、糯米粉、色膏、防腐用品、蜂蜜、甘油等为原料，借助拨子、滚子、切刀、梳板等工具，用手工搓条、拨花、展片、压滚珠、搓花条等造型技巧来塑造形象。作品格调上保持了韵味十足的传统特色，具有造型简练生动、形象逼真传神、比例夸张适当、色彩艳丽单纯的特点，富有浓厚的民间特色。

1959年7月，董凤岐考入北京中央工艺美术学院汤子博面塑工作室，学习了素描、图案、国画及中外美术史等专业课程，为面塑制作打下了良好的基础。1963年，被分配到沈阳美术设计公司与山东面人李芳阁同室工作，进行展览设计、沙盘模型及面塑研究创作。1983年，调入山东工艺美术学院后，专注从事面塑研究创作。

在从事面塑工作50余年期间，董凤岐继承了面塑的传统工艺，并加以创新，形成了自己的独特风格。用面粉捏塑的人物技巧纯熟、刻画精细、敷色艳丽、结构准确，面部表情真实传神、细腻，人物干净利落，造型准确。董凤岐擅长捏塑古典人物及现实生活中各类人物，具有通俗而不媚俗、富丽而不失典雅的风格特点，既有传统绘画风韵神采，又继承了面塑传统的各种表现形式与技艺的特色，完成了传统与现实的完美结合。董凤岐制作的核桃面人，头部有如绿豆大小，全身不到1厘米，面部表情却很传神，黑白眼珠分明，五官端正，色彩明亮。比如她创作的十八罗汉动态各异，有的怒目瞪视，有的慈目仰望，造型生动形象。

董凤岐担任山东工艺美术学院副教授期间，勤于教学，努力让更多的学生认识这项传统技艺，从而使其更好传承下去。2010年10月，在参与首届中国非物质文化遗产展览会期间，其面塑作品受到广大群众喜爱，也让更多人认识了面塑，为面塑传承发展做出了重要贡献。

Dong Fengqi—
Inheritor of Jinan Dough Sculpture

Dong Fengqi, female, born in 1939, is a Beijing native. She is a master of arts and crafts and a master of traditional skills in Shandong Province.

Jinan Dough Sculpture is made of flour, glutinous rice powder, color paste, preservatives, honey, glycerin and other raw materials. With the help of poker, roller, cutting knife, comb clapper and other tools, it uses hand-rubbing, drawing, exhibition, rolling balls, rubbing strips and other modeling techniques to shape the image. The style of the work maintains the traditional characteristics of full charm, with concise shapes and vivid images, exaggerated proportions, bright and simple colors, which has rich folk style.

In July 1959, Dong Fengqi was admitted to Tangzibo Dough Sculpture Studio of Beijing Central Academy of Arts and Crafts. She studied sketch, pattern, traditional Chinese painting and history of Chinese and foreign art, which laid a good foundation for her later dough sculpture creation. In 1963, she was assigned to Shenyang Art Design Company and became the colleague of the Shandong Dough Sculpture artist Li Fangge, to engage in exhibition design, and sand table model and dough sculpture research and creation. After being transferred to Shandong University of Arts and Design in 1983, she became dedicated to the research and creation of dough sculpture.

Dong Fengqi inherited the traditional technology of dough sculpture and created her own unique style during more than 50 years of work in dough sculpture. The characters made of flour by her are skilled, fine in description, brilliant in color application, accurate in structure, true and vivid in facial expression, delicate, clean and neat in character and accurate in shape. Dong Fengqi is good at classical characters and all kinds of characters in real life. In style, it is popular but not vulgar, rich and elegant. It not only has the charm of traditional painting, but also inherits the characteristics of various forms and techniques of traditional dough sculpture, thus achieving the perfect combination of tradition and reality. Her walnut dough sculpture has a head as small as a mungbean and a body less than 1 cm. However, the facial expressions are vivid. They have clear black and white eyes, good facial features and bright colors. For example, the eighteen Arhats created by her have different acts: some stare with anger, some look up with kindness, but all of them are vivid.

While Dong Fengqi was an associate professor of Shandong University of Arts and Design, she was diligent in teaching, so that more students could understand this traditional skill and that it could be better inherited. In October 2010, in the First Intangible Cultural Heritage Exhibition, her dough sculptures were admired by the general public, and helped more people to understand dough sculpture, making an important contribution to the inheritance and development of dough sculpture.

阳谷木雕传承人——王传成

王传成，男，1954 年出生，山东阳谷人，齐鲁文化之星，山东省民间手工艺制作大师。

阳谷县地处鲁西平原，隶属中国江北水城——聊城市，是运河文化、黄河文化、水浒文化的交融之地，为民间美术、传统工艺的留存提供了文化土壤。阳谷木雕是阳谷县的特色工艺之一，以诸子百家故事、儒佛道经典故事、历史故事等为题材，具有内涵丰富、线条豪放、造型大气的特点。

王传成出生于阳谷木雕世家，从小便喜爱传统文化和木雕木刻。在 20 世纪六七十年代，王传成雕刻红色版画和领袖像，到八九十年代雕工艺品、家具花板和木版画。1990 年，王传成创办文化家具研究所后，开始专注研究阳谷木雕这一传统工艺。

在继承阳谷木雕技艺传统工艺流程的基础上，即备料、干燥、下料、描图、粗雕、精雕、涂饰七个步骤，王传成不断完善发展。创作的木雕主要有三大系列：一是工艺品，包括实用类，如笔筒、印章等，以及装饰类，如屏风、壁挂、艺术摆件等；二是家具，包括行业家具和文化家具；三是木刻版画，如清代小说插图版画、民国期间抗日版画等。制作的阳谷木雕文化内涵丰富，具有鲜明的地方人文气息。其作品多次获国家及省、市级奖项。2012 年 10 月，其创作的《状元书房家具》在济南举办的第四届中国工艺精品博览会上获金奖。

保护不忘传承，王传成之子王志达在父亲的悉心传授下，将传统木雕手艺和优秀文化结合，创作了一批具有鲜明特色的木刻版画、工艺品和文化家具。同时，王传成协助其子扩大木雕作坊，提高生产效率，促进了这一传统工艺的传播，为阳谷木雕的传承做出了重要贡献。

Wang Chuancheng—Inheritor of Yanggu Wood Carving

Wang Chuancheng, male, born in 1954, is a native of Yanggu County, Shandong Province, a Star of Qilu Culture and a master of folk crafts in Shandong Province.

Yanggu County, located in the western plain of Shandong Province, is subordinate to Liaocheng, a water city in the north of the Yangtze River in China. It is a place blending canal culture, Yellow River culture and Water Margin culture. It provides a cultural soil for the preservation of folk art and traditional crafts. Yanggu Wood Carving is one of the special crafts in Yanggu County. It takes the stories of hundreds of schools of thought, Confucianism, Buddhism and Taoism, and historical stories as its subject matters. It is characterized by rich cultural connotation, bold lines and grand modeling.

Wang Chuancheng was born in a Yanggu wood carving family. He has been fond of traditional culture and wood carving since his childhood. In the 1960s and 1970s, Wang Chuancheng carved red prints and the leaders' portraits, and in the 1980s and 1990s he carved crafts, furniture and woodcut prints. After Wang Chuancheng founded the Institute of Cultural Furniture in 1990, he began to focus on the traditional craft of Yanggu Wood Carving.

Wang Chuancheng inherited the traditional process of Yanggu Wood Carving, and improved and developped the seven steps, namely material preparation, drying, blanking, drawing, rough carving, fine carving and painting. He created three main series of wood carvings. One is handicraft, including practical products such as penholders, seals, and decorative products such as screens, wall hangings, art ornaments, and so on. Another is furniture, including industrial furniture and cultural furniture. The other is woodcut prints, including illustrations of novels in the Qing Dynasty, anti-Japanese prints and so on. The Yanggu woodcarvings made by him have rich cultural connotations and distinct local humanistic flavors. His works have won many national and provincial and municipal awards. Among them *Furniture in Zhuangyuan's Study* won the gold medal in the fourth China Craft Exhibition held in Jinan in October 2012.

Wang Zhida, the son of Wang Chuancheng, combined traditional woodcarving techniques with excellent culture and created a number of woodcarving prints, handicrafts and cultural furnitures with distinctive characteristics under his father's careful instruction. At the same time, Wang Chuancheng helped his son expand the wood carving workshop, improve production efficiency, promoting the spread of this traditional craft and making an important contribution to the inheritance of Yanggu Wood Carving.

潍县布玩具传承人——孙秀兰

孙秀兰，女，1978 年出生，山东潍坊人，潍坊市首批民间艺术大师。

潍县布玩具最早起源于绣房中少女、少妇用碎布片做成的小人儿，俗称“针姑子”。其制作的原材料是各色布料、彩线及白乳胶等，具有设计随意、因材成形的特点。潍县布玩具的造型十分夸张，各种动物的艺术形象都妙在“似与不似”之间。在色彩上，潍县布玩多使用红、蓝、黄、绿、黑等色彩，形成了鲜明、强烈的艺术风格，极具民间乡土气息。

孙秀兰在母亲的影响下，自幼爱好布玩具设计和制作。1993 从学校毕业后，她正式跟随母亲孙爱美学习潍县布玩具的制作。2003 年，成立了自己的布玩具作坊，开始专注研究潍县布玩具的制作技艺。2008 年，为扩大生产规模，孙秀兰成立了自己的布玩具厂，将潍县布玩具发展成现在的几百甚至几千个品种。

传统潍县布玩具一般以棉布为主，辅以彩色丝绸、绢缎、绒布、皮毛、彩线、金银线、空心珠等装饰材料，经过复杂细致的手工缝制而成。孙秀兰在继承传统工艺的基础上，融入现代艺术元素，使作品更富有现代感，同时能根据中国的传统风俗与生肖设计相关作品，民间意味浓厚，深受老百姓的喜爱。

为保护传承这一传统技艺，孙秀兰每周都会到学校去，指导孩子们自己动手设计、制作布玩具，激发孩子们的学习兴趣。孙秀兰的作品也得到了社会各界的认可，多项作品获国家及省、市级奖项。其设计的“手绣大狮子”被评为法国巴黎举办的中法文化年吉祥物；“狮子滚绣球”在全国工艺美术展览会上被评为 10 种优秀产品之一，被邮电部选定为纪念邮票图案。其作品被众多国内外媒体报道，不仅促进了潍县布玩具的传播与传承，而且也让更多人了解到了这一民间优秀传统工艺。

Sun Xiulan—Inheritor of Wei County Cloth Toys

Sun Xiulan, female, born in 1978, is a native of Weifang, Shandong Province, and belongs to the first batch of folk art masters in Weifang.

Wei County Cloth Toys originated from the little doll made by young girls and young women in embroidery houses from fragments of cloth, commonly known as the "sewn maid". Its raw materials are all kinds of cloth, colorful threads and white latex, etc. It has the characteristics of random design and forms according to the material. The shape of Wei County Cloth Toys is highly exaggerated, and the wonder of the artistic images of all kinds of animals lies in their "between like and unlike". The colors include red, blue, yellow, green, black, etc., forming a distinct, strong artistic style with a distinct folk flavor.

Sun Xiulan, under her mother's influence, has been fond of the design and production of cloth toys since her childhood. After graduating from school in 1993, she formally followed her mother Sun Aimei to study the handicraft of Wei County Cloth Toys. In 2003, she set up her own cloth toy workshop and started to focus on the production techniques of Wei County Cloth Toys. In 2008, in order to expand the production scale, Sun Xiulan set up her own cloth toy factory and developed hundreds or even thousands varieties of Wei County Cloth Toys.

Traditional Wei County Cloth Toys are mainly made of cotton cloth, colored silk, silk satin, velvet, fur, colored thread, gold and silver thread, hollow beads and other decorative materials, which are carefully sewn through complex and meticulous manual work. Sun Xiulan, on the basis of inheriting traditional crafts, has integrated modern art elements into her works. At the same time, Sun Xiulan can design works according to Chinese traditional customs, which has strong folk art flavor and is much appreciated by the people.

In order to protect and inherit this traditional skill, Sun Xiulan goes to school every week to direct children design and make cloth toys by themselves and stimulate children's interest in learning. Sun Xiulan's works have also been recognized by all walks of life, and many of them have won national and provincial and municipal awards. Her work "Hand-embroidered Big Lion" was chosen as the mascot of the Year of Sino-French Cultural Exchange in Paris, France. Her work "Lion Rolling Embroidery Ball" was selected as one of the 10 excellent products at the National Arts and Crafts Exhibition and selected as the design of commemorative stamps by the Ministry of Posts and Telecommunications. Her works are reported by many domestic and foreign media, which not only promotes the spread and inheritance of Wei County Cloth Toys, but also make more people understand this excellent traditional folk craft.

傳承人

〈 山东省省级非物质文化遗产项目 〉
代表性传承人

第四卷

传统技艺

Traditional Artistry

潍坊风筝传承人——张效东

张效东，男，1949年出生，山东潍坊寒亭区人，潍坊工艺美术大师。

潍坊风筝兴于明初，盛于清代。它以造型丰富、结构合理、色彩艳丽、起飞高稳、富有民间乡土气息的特色而自成一家。潍坊风筝在初期以板子风筝为主，后经过演变，逐步形成了以硬翅风筝为主、长串“蜈蚣”为最、软翅风筝为巧、筒子风筝为奇的体系。随着潍坊国际风筝节的举办，潍坊风筝的发展达到鼎盛时期。

8岁时，张效东师承著名风筝老艺人杨同科先生，跟随师傅学习泥塑雕刻，扎制风筝，是潍坊风筝扎制技艺第五代传人。1986年，创办风筝厂，潜心钻研，继承并创新潍坊风筝制作技艺。张效东在传统的样式基础上加以改进和创新，尝试利用齿轮的机械原理制作会动的新式风筝。几次试验后，张效东终于做成了会动的翼龙风筝。张效东在翼龙的肚子里设计安装了一个连着导杆的风轮，风一吹，风轮就开始转动，带动导杆上下左右摇动，从而使翼龙的两只眼睛可以左右眨动，舌头可以进出伸缩，前爪可以自由挥动，令人叫绝，使风筝变成了活的工艺品。

同时，张效东在祖辈流传下来的传统风筝扎制技艺的基础上不断改革。他在风筝的扎制上注重骨架结构与主题内容的协调新颖；在风筝的特点上保持了潍坊风筝的传统特色；在选材和色彩上，借鉴了潍坊年画和民间泥塑、老虎玩具的装饰美。张效东将声、光、电等科技元素融入传统风筝扎制工艺中，形成了不同的风格体系。

张效东在风筝创新和传播方面做出了重要贡献。到目前为止，他已经为潍坊风筝创新品种百余个，传授技艺百余人，先后被授予“潍坊工艺美术大师”“潍坊民间文化杰出传承人”等称号。其作品多次在潍坊国际风筝节上获得创新扎制金奖、银奖、铜奖等各种奖项。其中，优秀的风筝作品有《翼龙》《马踏飞燕》《神州五号》《锣鼓喧天迎奥运风筝》《花开中国》等。

Zhang Xiaodong—Inheritor of Weifang Kites

Zhang Xiaodong, male, born in 1949, Hanting District, Weifang, Shandong Province, is a master of arts and crafts in Weifang.

Weifang Kites originated in the early Ming Dynasty and thrived in the Qing Dynasty. It developed its own style of plentiful shapes, reasonable structure, brilliant colors, high and stable takeoff, and rich folk local flavor. Weifang Kites in the initial stage were plate kites, then through evolution gradually formed a system of hard-wing kite as mainstream, long string "centipedes" as the most, soft-wing kites as artifice, tube kites as oddness. With the holding of Weifang International Kite Festival, Weifang kites has reached its peak.

At the age of 8, Zhang Xiaodong learned clay sculpture and kite making from his teacher. He was apprenticed to the famous old kite artist Mr. Yang Tongke, one of the fifth-generation inheritors of the kite making skills in Yangjiabu. In 1986, he founded the kite factory, devoted himself to the research, inherited and innovated Weifang Kites production skills. Zhang Xiaodong improved and innovated on the basis of the traditional style. He tried to use the mechanical principle of gears to make a new type of animated kite. After several experiments, Zhang Xiaodong finally made an animated pterosaur kite. He designed and installed a wind wheel connected with a guide rod in the belly of the pterosaur. When the wind blew, the wind wheel started to rotate, driving the guide rod up and down and left and right, so that the pterosaur's eyes could blink, tongue could expand and retract, forepaw could move freely, which amazingly made the kite an animated handicraft.

Meanwhile, Zhang Xiaodong keeps reforming the traditional kite-binding techniques handed down from his ancestors. In the tie-up of kites, attention has been paid to the coordination and novelty of the skeleton structure and theme content. In the characteristics of Kites, the traditional characteristics of Weifang kites have been maintained. In the selection of materials and colors, the decorative beauty of Weifang New Year Pictures, folk clay sculptures and tiger toys has been used for reference. Zhang Xiaodong integrated sound, light, electricity and other scientific and technological elements into the traditional kite tie-up process, forming a different style system.

Zhang Xiaodong have made important contributions to kite innovation and dissemination. Up to now, he has brought forth more than one hundred new types of Weifang kites, and has taught more than one hundred people the skills. He has been awarded the title of Weifang Master of Arts and Crafts, Weifang Outstanding Inheritor of Folk Culture and so on. His works participated in the Weifang International Kite Festival and won various honors such as gold, silver and bronze prizes for innovation. His masterpieces include *Pterosaur*, *Stepping Horse and Flying Swallow*, *Shenzhou No. 5*, *Gongs and Drums Greet the Olympic Games*, *Flowering China*, etc.

鲁西南民间织锦技艺传承人——刘春英

刘春英，女，1965年出生，山东郓城人。

鲁西南民间织锦简称“鲁锦”，又称“山东织花布”“花格子布”，是山东省独有的一种民间纯棉手工纺织品，目前主要集中于鲁西南和鲁北地区。鲁锦工艺有700多年的历史，早在元明之际就形成了独特的鲁西南棉布。随着纺织机械的更新和化工染料的应用，鲁锦工艺达到了炉火纯青的境界，织造的花布曾被作为贡品进献朝廷，成为大内御用之物。鲁锦常用的颜色有大红、桃红、湖蓝、靛青、绿、棕、紫、白、黑、黄等，采用天然的植物染料染色，不仅色谱齐全，而且绿色环保。

刘春英自幼跟随母亲刘凤莲学习鲁锦技艺，并且很快掌握了织造技术。刘春英最擅长的是提花织锦。提花织锦通常用四片综织造，刘春英则可以使用六片综织造鲁锦，其织锦花纹的复杂和丰富的表现力远远胜过四片综的鲁锦。在长期的摸索实践中，刘春英不断创新、改进鲁锦织造技艺，逐渐形成了现代鲁锦融提花、打花、挑花工艺于一体的独特风格。通过不断的探索，她将产品的纹样由最初的斜纹、条纹发展出枣花纹、水纹、合斗纹等多种较为复杂的纹样，并通过抽象图纹的重复、平行、连续、间隔、对比等变化来体现图案意境，极具艺术魅力。

刘春英掌握的织锦技艺精湛，技法多样，除提花外她还熟练地掌握了包花、砍花、打花以及通经断纬等织造技法。织造的鲁锦具有图案精致古雅、色彩绚丽、品种繁多、质地细密、舒适耐用的特点，具有鲜明的地方特色。

2011年，刘春英参加了山东工艺美院在北京中国美术馆举办的“手艺农村”展览，现场演示鲁锦织造技艺，获得观众的广泛好评。2012年，她跟随鲁锦织造技艺的保护单位——郓城县鲁锦工艺品有限责任公司参加中国非物质文化遗产博览会，荣获传承人奖。

Liu Chunying—Inheritor of Southwest Shandong Folk Brocade Craft

Liu Chunying, female, was born in Juancheng County, Shandong Province in 1965.

The folk brocade in southwest Shandong is called "Lu Brocade" for short. It is also called Shandong woven flower cloth or plaid cloth. It is a kind of folk pure cotton handicraft textiles unique to Shandong Province. At present, it mainly locates at southwest and north Shandong. Lu Brocade has a history of more than 700 years. As early as the Yuan and Ming Dynasties, it formed a unique cotton cloth in southwest Shandong. With the renewal of textile machinery and the application of chemical dyestuffs, the Lu Brocade technology has attained perfection in art and skills. The woven flower cloth was once offered as a tribute to the court and became dedicated to the imperial court. The commonly used colors of Lu Brocade include bright red, peach red, light blue, indigo, green, brown, purple, white, black and yellow, etc. The natural plant dyes are used for dyeing, which not only have complete chromatograms, but also are green and environmentally friendly.

Liu Chunying followed her mother Liu Fenglian at her childhood to learn the skills of Lu Brocade, and quickly mastered the weaving technology. Liu Chunying excels in jacquard brocade the most. Jacquard brocade is usually made of four pieces of composite weaving. Liu Chunying uses six pieces of composite weaving to make Lu Brocade, whose complexity and rich expression in pattern are far better than these of the Lu Brocade made of the four pieces of composite weaving. In the long-term exploration and practice, Liu Chunying constantly innovates and improves the weaving skills of Lu Brocade, and gradually forms a unique style of modern Lu Brocade which integrates jacquard weave, tuck stitch, and cross stitch techniques. Through constant exploration, the pattern of the product has been developed from the original twill and stripe to a variety of more complex patterns, such as jujube pattern, water pattern and combo pattern. The artistic conception of the pattern is embodied through the repetition, parallelism, continuity, spacing and contrast of the abstract pattern, which is of great artistic charm.

Liu Chunying has mastered exquisite brocade skills and various techniques. Besides jacquard, she has mastered the weaving techniques of surrounding stitch, cutting stitch, tuck stitch, and pass warp and cut weft. Her works of Lu Brocade are characterized by exquisite and elegant pattern, gorgeous color, various varieties, fine texture, comfort and durability, and have distinct local characteristics.

In 2011, Liu Chunying participated in the "Handicraft Countryside" Exhibition held by Shandong Academy of Arts and Crafts in Beijing China Art Museum, demonstrating Lu Brocade weaving skills on the spot, and won wide acclaim from the audience. In 2012, following the Lu Brocade weaving technology protection unit—Juancheng County Lujin Handicraft Co., Ltd., she participated in China Intangible Cultural Heritage Exposition, and won the inheritor award.

郓城古筝制作技艺传承人——刁兆玉

刁兆玉，男，1943年出生，山东郓城人。

古筝是一种中国传统乐器中的弹拨乐器，是我国重要的民族乐器之一。郓城古筝制作技艺是与古筝名家紧密相连的，具有“齐鲁大板”之称的山东筝是我国古筝演奏八大流派之一。郓城制筝作坊产生于明代洪武年间，创始人是刁琅。后经历代传承，由原来的16弦，增加至16弦、18弦、21弦、23弦、26弦五个品种系列，可演奏的音域更加宽广。

刁兆玉生于古筝制作世家，从小耳濡目染，学习古筝制作技艺，是郓城古筝制作技艺的第二十四代传人。刁兆玉自1963年师从刁秀欣学习制作古筝，学习期满后在郓城镇刁东村古筝厂开始制作古筝。2007年，被水浒好汉城古筝坊聘为专职技师，从事古筝制作工作至今。

刁兆玉制作的古筝采用优质桐木为原料，经过阴干和烘烤等传统工序，全部手工制作，外形美观大方，音域宽广，具有高音明亮而不燥、低音纯厚而不空、余音悠长而不浊的特点。高、中、低音区音色平均，既善于表现优美抒情的曲调，又能演奏气势磅礴的乐章，深受国内外古筝弹奏家喜爱。

郓城古筝一直受到各地筝乐演奏家的登门求购，刁兆玉曾亲自为全国著名古筝演奏家山东艺术学院教授韩庭贵、西安音乐学院教授高自成、美籍华人张燕等制造古筝。中国东方歌舞团、中国人民解放军文工团、中国音乐学院等著名文艺团体也都使用他制作的古筝。自20世纪80年代初开始，郓城古筝走出了国门，远销美国、日本、新加坡、韩国等十几个国家和地区。多年以来，刁兆玉又先后培养了多名古筝制作继承人，使郓城古筝的制作技艺得以完整传承，为郓城古筝制作的繁荣和发展做出了重要贡献。

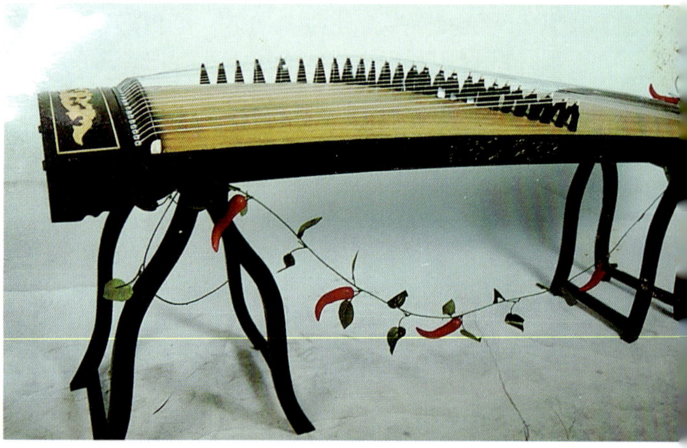

Diao Zhaoyu—Inheritor of Yuncheng Guzheng Craft

Diao Zhaoyu, male, was born in Yuncheng County, Shandong Province in 1943.

Guzheng is a plucked stringed instrument among traditional Chinese musical instrument and an important folk musical instrument of China. The craft of Yuncheng Guzheng has much to do with famous Guzheng artists. Shandong Guzheng, known as "Qilu Daban" (in Chinese Pinyin), is one of the eight major schools of Guzheng playing in China. Yuncheng Guzheng Workshop came into being in the Hongwu Reigh of the Ming Dynasty. Its founder was Diao Lang. Passed on from generation to generation, it developed from the original 16 strings to the later five series of 18 strings, 21 strings, 23 strings, etc. and the tone range became broader.

Diao Zhaoyu was born in a family of Guzheng craft. He has been influenced since an early age and began to learn the production craft of Guzheng when he was a child. He is the twenty-fourth generation inheritor of Yuncheng Guzheng craft. Diao Zhaoyu started to learn Guzheng craft from Diao Xiuxin in 1963, and began making Guzheng at the Guzheng Factory of Diaodong Village in Yuncheng Town after his study. In 2007, he was employed as a full-time technician, and has been engaged in the production of Guzheng till now.

Diao Zhaoyu's Guzheng is all handmade and is made from high-quality paulownia wood through traditional processes such as shade drying and baking, with beautiful and elegant appearance and wide range of sound. It has the characteristics of wide tone range. The high pitch is bright but not harsh, the bass pitch is pure but not empty, and the lingering sound is long but not dull. The average timbre of the high, middle and bass areas is capable of expressing beautiful lyric melodies and visualizing powerful movements, and is much favored by the Guzheng players both at home and abroad.

Yuncheng Guzheng has been purchased personally by Guzheng musicians from all over the country. Diao Zhaoyu has made Guzheng in person for famous Guzheng performers such as Han Tinggui, Professor of Shandong University of Arts, Gao Zicheng, Professor of Xi'an Conservatory of Music, and Zhang Yan, a Chinese American. His Guzheng works have also been chosen by such well-known art groups nationwide as China Dongfang Song and Dance Troupe, PLA General Political Department Art Troupe, China Conservatory of Music, etc. Since the early 1980s, Yuncheng Guzheng has been exported to more than a dozen countries and areas such as the United States, Japan, Singapore and Korea, etc. Over the years, Diao Zhaoyu has cultivated many inheritors of Yuncheng Guzheng craft, strengthening the inheritance process. He has made remarkable contribution to the prosperity and development of Yuncheng Guzheng craft.

柳疃丝绸技艺传承人——魏耀琳

魏耀琳，男，1954 年出生，山东昌邑柳疃镇人，昌邑市华裕丝绸有限责任公司董事长兼总经理。

柳疃丝绸指茧绸，即柞绸，又称“山东绸”或“鲁绸”。昌邑市柳疃镇是山东省著名的“丝绸之乡”，历史上，人们把这里生产的丝绸称为“柳绸”。柳疃丝绸业始于清代。道光年间，柳疃人发明了木制脚踏纩车，柞蚕缫丝技艺不断提高，产品质量不断改进，远销到北京，这种柞绸被称作“柳疃绸”。清末民初，柳疃丝绸业发展到鼎盛时期，大约从 1916 年起开始走向衰落。

魏耀琳于 1974 年到昌邑县丝织一厂当学徒，经过刻苦学艺，熟练地掌握了泡丝、络丝、浆丝、织造等丝绸制作技艺。由于技术出众，工作成绩突出，他先后担任车间技术员、车间主任、副厂长等职务，2002 年起担任昌邑市华裕丝有限责任公司董事长。

魏耀琳不仅熟悉柳疃丝绸技艺的每一道工序，而且了解每一道工序应该注意的关键技术。其生产的丝绸产品粗犷而不失细腻，具有独特的风格特点。魏耀琳根据市场需要，对各道工序操作和生产工艺进行了改进，漂炼压光后，丝绸外观美丽，手感柔软，穿着舒适。同时，他还制定了详细的操作流程和织造技术标准：要求泡丝泡透，晾丝内外干湿均匀一致；络丝张力大小一致，成型良好；并丝不少股，不刹边；整经张力一致，不掉头，不错绞;织造减少断头，不顶绞、不底漏、不差花、边道好。解决了长期影响产品质量的紧经、亮条等病疵。魏耀琳还成功开发了每平米 15 克的轻薄真丝雪纺产品和每平方米 200 克的重磅真丝双面绉产品，其每年研发的新产品达 50 余种。

魏耀琳参与研制的真丝产品曾获多个奖项。其中，颖花绉及真丝砂洗系列产品获山东省科技进步奖，还获得多项山东省优秀新产品奖和潍坊市科技进步奖。他长期坚持收徒授艺，建立了柳疃丝绸技艺传习所，先后培养了几十名传承人，使柳疃丝绸传统技艺得到了很好的传承。

Wei Yaolin—Inheritor of Liutuan Silk Craft

Wei Yaolin, male, born in 1954, is a native of Liutuan Town, Changyi City, Shandong Province. He is the board chairman and general manager of Huayu Silk Co., Ltd. of Changyi City.

Liutuan Silk belongs to cocoon silk, i.e. tussah silk, also known as "Shandong silk" or "Lu silk". Liutuan Town, Changyi City is a famous "silk town" in Shandong Province. In history, people called the Silk produced here "Liu silk". Liutuan Silk industry began in the Qing Dynasty. During the Daoguang Reign, Liutuan people invented wooden treadmill. The silk reeling skills of tussah silk were continuously improved, and the quality was constantly ameliorated. It was sold far to Beijing. This kind of tussah silk was called "Liutuan silk". During the late Qing Dynasty and the early Republic of China, the silk industry in Liutuan reached its peak. It began to decline around 1916.

Wei Yaolin came to Changyi County Silk Weaving Factory in 1974 to be an apprentice. Through hard work, he mastered such silk crafts as soaking, twining, sizing and weaving. Because of his outstanding skills and achievements, he has successively held the positions of workshop technician, workshop director, factory deputy director, etc. Since 2002, he has been the board chairman of Huayu Silk Co., Ltd. of Changyi City.

Wei Yaolin is familiar with every process of Liutuan silk craft, and he knows the noteworthy key technologies in the process of silk matching. His silk products are rough and delicate, with unique style. Wei Yaolin improved the operation and production technology of each process in accordance with the market demand. After the process of bleaching and calendering, the silk looks beautiful, feels soft and wears comfortable. Meanwhile, the detailed operation process and

weaving technical standards were formulated, which set requirements for thorough soaking, uniform drying, consistent twining tension and good shaping, strands of silk without loss and edge cutting, uniform warping tension with good twisting and no turning around, reduced broken ends, no top twisting, no bottom leakage, no pattern missed, and good sideways. It has overcome the long-term quality defects such as tight warp and bright strip, etc. Wei Yaolin has also successfully developed light silk chiffon products of 15 grams per square meter and heavy silk crepe products of 200 grams per square meter. Each year over 50 new kinds of silk products come into being through his research and development.

Wei Yaolin has won many awards for his research and development of silk products, such as Weifang Science and Technology Progress Award, Shandong Science and Technology Progress Award, and a number of other provincial excellent new product awards. He has persisted in apprenticing and teaching activities for a long time, cultivated dozens of inheritors successively in Liutuan Silk Craft Training Center that he founded, so that the traditional Liutuan Silk craft was well inherited.

景芝酒传统酿造技艺传承人——赵德义

赵德义，男，1967年出生，山东安丘景芝镇人，高级工程师。

景芝酒酿造工艺历史久远。明洪武年间，景芝镇酿酒规模已相当可观。景芝酒是采用传统工艺酿造的粮食酒，从原料的选择到制曲、发酵、蒸馏、贮藏等，每道工艺都有很多讲究。中华人民共和国成立后，景芝酿酒业开始了一个新纪元，“景芝白乾”荣获国家“大众名白酒”称号，深受大众喜爱。

赵德义出身于酿酒世家，自曾祖父赵梦武一代开始挖掘酿酒的传统技艺，后又经过祖父赵顺敬、父亲赵淑兴不断努力，将酿酒技艺不断改良并传授给赵德义。赵德义自1985年在山东景芝酒厂从事酿酒工作，现任山东景芝酒业股份有限公司总工程师。

景芝酒采用纯粮固态发酵，按传统工艺酿造而成。其传统技艺为：清蒸续渣，泥底砖窖，大麸结合，多微共酵，三高一长（高氮配料、高温堆积、高温发酵、长期贮存），精心勾调。在长期的传承实践中，形成了如下酿酒秘诀：“原料为当地产黑萼青茬高粱，这种高粱淀粉的角质率高，耐蒸煮，产酒好又多。辅料为谷壳”，粉碎呈“梅花瓣，无跑生”，配料要求“无团糟，无白眼”，入池发酵根据季节与气温变化，合理调整水分和酸度，装甑要“轻、松、匀、薄、准、平”，缓火蒸馏，大气追尾，糊化要“熟而不粘，内无生心”。

赵德义在研究传统酿酒技艺的基础上，创造了高端芝麻香型白酒，现已拥有多项发明专利和多项实用新型专利，其中“芝麻香型白酒生产工艺”荣获第十届山东省发明专利一等奖和第十二届中国专利优秀奖。多年来，他注重产、学、研、用相结合和技术人才的培养，通过理论与实践相结合的方式传授景芝酒传统酿造技艺，培养了多名专业技术带头人和技术骨干，对景芝酒传统酿酒技艺的传承和发展做出了突出贡献。

传统技艺

Zhao Deyi—Inheritor of Traditional Brewing Craft of Jingzhi Liquor

Zhao Deyi, male, born in 1967, is a senior engineer from Jingzhi Town, Anqiu, Shandong Province.

The brewing skill of Jingzhi Liquor has a long history. During the Hongwu Reign of the Ming Dynasty, the scale of liquor brewing in Jingzhi Town was already rather considerable. Jingzhi Liquor is a grain liquor brewed with traditional skill. From the choice of raw materials to koji making, fermentation, distillation, storage, etc, there are many fastidious skills in each process. After the foundation of the People's Republic of China, Jingzhi Liquor industry entered a new era. It won the national "popular liquor" title and was much favored by the public.

Zhao Deyi was born in a liquor brewing family. Since the generation of his great-grandfather Zhao Mengwu who began to explore the traditional skills of liquor brewing, and then through the continuous efforts of his grandfather Zhao Shunjing and his father Zhao Shuxing, the skills of liquor brewing have been continuously improved and then imparted to Zhao Deyi. Zhao Deyi has been working in Shandong Jingzhi Brewery since 1985. He is currently the chief engineer of Shandong Jingzhi Liquor Co., Ltd.

Jingzhi Liquor is brewed with solid-state fermentation of pure grains with traditional skill. Its traditional craft is characterized by separate steaming and mixed into cellar, mud bottom brick cellar, large bran combination, multi-micro co-fermentation, three high and one long (high nitrogen ingredients, high temperature accumulation, high temperature fermentation, long-term storage), and meticulous blending. The liquor-making secret has accumulated during the long-term inheritance practice as follows. "The raw materials should be the local produced black calyx green stubble sorghum, whose starch has

a high corniness, good cooking resistance, and produces good liquor abundantly. The auxiliary material is husk." The pulverized raw materials shall be "sporeless and like plum petals", and the ingredients are required to be "without cluster lees and white spots". Pond fermentation should be conducted according to seasonal and temperature changes, with reasonable adjustment of water and acidity. The steamer filling should be "light, loose, uniform, thin, accurate, and flat". The fire should be slow in distillation and great in ending. The cooked grain should be "thoroughly ripe but not sticky ".

Zhao Deyi has created high-end sesame-flavor liquor based on the research of traditional liquor craft. Now he owns many invention patents and utility model patents. Among them, the invention patent of "Sesame-flavor Liquor Production Skill" won the tenth Shandong Invention Patent First Prize and the Twelfth China Patent Excellence Award. Over the years, he paid attention to the combination of production, education, research, and application, and the cultivation of technical talents. Teaching Jingzhi Liquor traditional brewing techniques through theory and practice, he has trained a number of professional and technical leaders and technical backbones, and has made outstanding contributions to the inheritance and development of the traditional brewing craft of Jingzhi Liquor.

鲁菜烹饪技艺传承人——张吉顺

张吉顺，男，1948年出生，山东烟台福山人，鲁菜烹饪专家。

张吉顺在自身传承鲁菜烹饪技艺的同时，还言传身教带好徒弟，严格要求徒弟扎实练艺。几十年来他带出来的烹饪厨师有90余人。此外，他还积极倡导开展鲁菜烹饪技艺大比武活动，推动鲁菜烹饪技艺的广泛交流，互相学习，取长补短，扩大了“鲁菜之乡”的对外影响力及知名度。2002年6月，在首届中国（烟台）五彩缤纷国际美食节上，张吉顺烹制的热菜“清汤燕窝”获金奖，并获个人“中华美食大奖”。

鲁菜是胶东福山菜与济南历下菜、曲阜孔府菜的合璧，其重要支柱是以烹饪海鲜为代表的福山风味菜肴。福山鲁菜用料严格精细，烹饪技术精湛，技法全面，精于熘、爆、炸、扒、蒸、烧、炒、煸等，十分讲究刀工、火候和调味。经过精心烹饪后的福山菜肴，以“菜香不邪，食而不腻，原汤原味，鲜嫩为主，偏重清淡”著称于世。

张吉顺长期坚持工作在第一线。自1969年开始在济南军区政治部厨房担任炊事班长，1977~1984在烟台虹口宾馆担任厨师长，1985~1992在福山区华侨宾馆担任厨师长，2013至今在吉升馆餐饮管理有限公司担任董事长。在烹饪工作实践中，张吉顺虚心学习师傅王义均的烹饪高招，认真学习挖掘、研究、探讨福山鲁菜烹饪技艺，不断提高自己的烹饪技术。

从事烹饪工作40余年，张吉顺积累了丰富的烹饪和管理经验，对胶东风味的传统鲁菜烹调技法有深刻研究。他烹制的海鲜菜品色、香、味、形皆令人称道，其中以“味”为最。为使菜肴更适应现代群众饮食需要，张吉顺还组织挖掘地方风味小吃，丰富了鲁菜的内容。

Zhang Jishun—
Inheritor of Shandong Cuisine Culinary Skills

Zhang Jishun, male, born in Fushan District, Yantai, Shandong Province in 1948, is an expert in Shandong Cuisine.

Shandong Cuisine is a combination of Jiaodong Fushan Cuisine, Jinan Lixia Cuisine and Qufu Confucian Cuisine, of which Fushan Cuisine represented by seafood cooking is the dominant. Fushan Lu Cuisine is demanding and fine in ingredients, advanced in cooking technology and comprehensive in cooking skills. It is skilled in quick-frying, hot-frying, deep-frying, braising, steaming, braising, frying, stir-frying, etc. It is fastidious about knife work, fire duration and degree, and saucing. Through consummate cooking, Fushan Cuisine excels and becomes world-renowned for its "authentic flavor with original soup, fresh, tender, and mild taste, and no grease".

Zhang Jishun has been working in the front line for a long time. Since 1969, he has served as the head of the kitchen of Jinan Military Region's Political Department, as the chef of Hongkou Hotel in Yantai from 1977 to 1984, as the chef of Overseas Chinese Hotel in Fushan District from 1985 to 1992, and as the board chairman of Jisheng Restaurant Management Co., Ltd. since 2013. In the practice of cooking, Zhang Jishun modestly learned his master Wang Yijun's cooking skills, earnestly studied and explored, the cooking skills of Fushan Lu Cuisine, and constantly improved his cooking skills.

Zhang Jishun has been engaged in cooking for more than 40 years. He has accumulated rich experience in cooking and management. He has made a profound study of the traditional cooking techniques of Shandong Cuisine with Jiaodong flavor. His seafood dishes are praised for their color, aroma, taste and shape, among which taste ranks first. In order to make the dishes cater to the modern people's diet, Zhang Jishun also organized the exploration of local flavor snacks, which enriched the content of Shandong Cuisine.

Zhang Jishun not only inherited Shandong Cuisine's cooking skills in his own way, but also taught his apprentices carefully by his own words and deads. He set strict requirements, and required solid practice. Over the past decades, he has taught more than 90 cooks. In addition, he also actively advocated Shandong Cuisine cooking skills competition activities, and promoted the wide exchange of Shandong Cuisine cooking skills for cooks to learn from each other and make up for weaknesses, thus expanding the external influence and visibility of the "Shandong Cuisine Town". In June 2002, at the first China (Yantai) Colorful International Food Festival, Zhang Jishun's hot dish *Edible Bird's Nest in Clear Soup* got the gold medal and won him the "Chinese Food Award".

蓝印花布印染技艺传承人——相友文

相友文，男，1935年生，山东兰陵人。

蓝印花布最初以蓼蓝草中提取的靛蓝为染料，经过多重工艺，反复染色，才能达到所需颜色。蓝印花布的图案有的取材于百姓喜闻乐见的民间故事、戏曲、人物，有的则是由鸟兽鱼虫和花卉果蔬等组成的吉祥纹样，这些题材都与百姓的生活息息相关，很有乡土气息，令人倍感亲切。

相友文17岁就跟随祖父相敬伦学习布染技艺，现已是第四代传承人。相敬伦的“蝴蝶花瓶”“喜鹊闹梅”等床帏子作品，图案淳朴艳丽，广受欢迎。相友文痴迷于这一传统工艺，自1957年高小毕业后，便一直从事蓝印花布生意。每逢村镇集市，他便接受农户的来料加工，根据农户的需求印制各种花布。

在传承大仲村蓝印花布印染技艺的基础上，相友文还不断谋求创新发展。他自行设计了多种纹样，自刻印版，如“猫蹄花”“梅花鹿”“福字兜兜”等，深受老百姓喜爱。至20世纪90年代初，随着人们物质生活的改善和审美情趣的提高，相友文受到国家级和省市级多位专家教授的影响和指导，创作刻制了一部分新颖别致的纹样，如“红鱼戏莲”（韩美林设计）、“富贵花瓶”（叶又新设计）。他制作的蓝印花布纹样丰富，淳厚朴实，形象生动，具有较高的审美价值。此外，他还由单面印花发展到双面印花，形成了淳朴简洁、古朴素雅的艺术风格，部分作品还被中国美术馆及宋庆龄基金会等组织机构收藏。

1997年7月，在苍山县委宣传部主办的“迎香港回归”民间艺术品展览上，相友文的蓝印花布作品获得一等奖。2010年10月，相友文参加首届中国非物质文化遗产博览会并获得优秀传承人纪念奖。2012年9月，他参加第二届中国非物质文化遗产博览会并获得优秀传承人纪念奖。

Xiang Youwen—Inheritor of Printing and Dyeing Craft of Blue Printed Cloth

Xiang Youwen, male, was born in Lanling County, Shandong Province in 1935.

Blue printed cloth was originally made of indigo extracted from polygonum sibiricum. Through multiple processes and repeated dyeing, it can achieve the required color. Blue printed cloth patterns are based on popular folk stories, operas, characters, and auspicious manuscripts of birds, animals, fish, insects, flowers, fruits and vegetables. These themes are closely related to common people's lives and permeated by a local flavor, which makes people feel more intimate.

Xiang Youwen, now the fourth generation inheritor, learned the cloth dyeing craft at the age of 17 from his grandfather Xiang Jinglun, whose bed mat works such as *Butterfly Vase* and *Magpies Play Plums* are very popular for their simple and beautiful designs. Since graduating from the primary school (Gaoxiao in Chinese Pinyin) in 1957, Xiang Youwen has been engaged in blue printed cloth business. During every village fair, he received the raw materials from farmers and printed various kinds of designs according to their needs.

On the basis of inheriting the printing and dyeing skills of blue printed cloth in Dazhong Village, Xiang Youwen has been seeking innovative development. He designed a variety of patterns, and engraved original printing plates, such as *Cat Hoof Flower, Sika Deer, Fu Character Bellyband,* etc., which are popular with the people. At the beginning of the 1990s, with the improvement of people's material life and aesthetic taste, Xiang Youwen was influenced and directed by many experts and professors at the national, provincial and municipal levels. Some of his novel and unique patterns were created and carved, such as *Red Fish Playing Lotus* (Han Meilin Design) and *Rich and Precious Vase* (Ye Youxin Design). His patterns are abundant, honest and plain, vivid and rich in high aesthetic value. In addition, he developed one-sided printing to two-sided printing, forming his plain, succinct, unadorned and elegant artistic style. Some of his works are collected by Chinese Art Museum and Song Qingling Foundation and other organizations.

In July 1997, at the folk art exhibition with the theme of "Welcoming the Return of Hong Kong" sponsored by Cangshan Propaganda Bureau, Xiang Youwen's blue printed cloth works won the first prize. In October 2010, Xiang Youwen won the Excellent Inheritor Memorial Award at the First China Intangible Cultural Heritage Exposition, and in September 2012, at the second exposition he won the same award.

威海锡镶制作技艺传承人——谷祖威

谷祖威，男，1944年生，山东威海人。

锡镶技艺包括冶炼、铸制、锻打、镂雕、焊接等制作过程。威海锡镶技艺制作的作品大多是茶具、镶手杖、高级花瓶、钓鱼竿、奶罐、糖罐、白水罐、清水碗、奖杯、纪念品等与人们生活息息相关的作品。其艺术图案设计雕镂清晰，艺术形象生动、逼真，成为人们日常生活不可多得的实用艺术品。

谷祖威自幼学习锡镶技术。20世纪80年代，为适应对外开放的新形势，谷祖威积极发掘传统产品，重操父业，开办锡镶工艺品厂。他找出家藏的雕刻和成型工具，聘请已退休的当年新合成老技工担任技术顾问，克服了重重困难，终于在两三个月内试制成功。北京颐和园绘画馆工艺品部先后购进了100多件他制作的“威海卫锡壶”。1985年9月，他的一部分锡镶产品还被送往澳大利亚国际博览会展销。谷祖威还在传承的基础上发展创新，生产的产品除了茶具类品种外，又增加了镶手杖、高级花瓶、钓鱼竿等。在图案设计上，谷祖威也有突破。他设计的“八仙过海”等各种古代人物图案，格调健康文雅，从而使这一优秀的民间工艺重放异彩。

在传承这一传统技艺时，谷祖威精益求精。从锡镶工艺来看，茶具的镶饰部位讲究，锡片图案美观。如茶壶多镶饰在壶嘴、壶身、壶盖、壶颈处。壶盖图案为五蝠（福）捧寿、喜鹊登梅之类，壶盖中间的气孔是专门用光绪铜币压铸上去的；壶身图案多为双龙戏珠、龙凤呈祥、松鹤延年等。这些都是纯手工加工技艺，十分精致，艺术图案雕镂清晰，传神逼真。

谷祖威传承古老的锡镶制作技艺，极富胶东民间艺术特色。1986年，谷祖威荣获国家专利局颁发的锡镶工艺专利，其作品还曾获山东省第一届旅游纪念品二等奖。

Gu Zuwei—Inheritor of Weihai Tin Inlay Craft

Gu Zuwei, male, born in 1944, is from Weihai, Shandong Province.

Tin inlay craft covers smelting, casting, forging, carving, welding and other production processes. Most of Weihai Tin Inlay works are closely related to people's lives, such as tea sets, canes, high-grade vases, fishing rods, milk cans, sugar cans, white water cans, clear water bowls, trophies, souvenirs, etc. Because of its clear artistic design, vivid and lifelike artistic image, it is a rare practical work of art in people's daily life.

Gu Zuwei has been learning tin inlay technology since his childhood. In the 1980s, in order to adapt to the new situation of opening to the outside world, Gu Zuwei actively explored traditional products, restored his father's business, and set up tin-inlaid handicraft factories. He found out the tools for sculpture and molding in home collection, hired retired new synthetic old mechanics to serve as technical consultants, overcame many difficulties, and finally succeeded in trial production within two to three months. Beijing Summer Palace Art Museum Arts and Crafts Department has bought more than 100 Weihai Tin Pots made by him. In September 1985, some of his tin-inlaid products were sent to the Australian International Exposition for sale. Gu Zuwei also develops and innovates his technology on the basis of inheritance. Besides tea sets, he also produces inlaid sticks, high-grade vases, fishing rods and so on. Breaking through the limit of the old content, he designed a variety of ancient figures and other patterns, such as "eight immortals across the sea" with healthy and elegant style, thus making this excellent folk craft brilliant once again.

In inheriting this traditional skill, Gu Zuwei is careful and meticulous. From the perspective of tin inlay, the decorative parts of tea sets are fastidious, and the patterns of tin sheets are beautiful. For example, teapots are mostly inlaid on the spout, body, cover and neck. The drawings of the pot cover include *Five Bats* (fu in Chinese Pinyin) *Holding Longevity* and *Magpies Climbing Plums*, etc. The stomata in the middle of the pot cover is die cast by special Guangxu copper coin. The drawings of the pot body are mostly "Double Dragons Play Pearl" "Prosperity Brought by the Dragon and the Phoenix" "Longevity Crane", etc. These pure handicraft techniques are exquisite, and these artistic design carvings are clear and lifelike.

Gu Zuwei inherits the ancient tin inlay craft extremely rich in Jiaodong folk art features. In 1986, Gu Zuwei was awarded a tin inlay craft patent issued by the State Patent Office. His works also won the second prize of the first tourism souvenir in Shandong Province.

聊城牛筋腰带制作技艺传承人——张元杰

张元杰，男，1964 年出生，山东聊城人。

牛筋腰带，又称“凉带”，是东昌府区独有的一种纯手工民间传统工艺品。该产品选用鲁西优质牛皮、牛筋为原料，完全按照传统工艺，经过选料、刮毛、割皮、水浸、编织、整形、轧光、上漆、配钎等十几道工序精心手工制作而成，以花纹细腻、色泽美观而著称。它还具有清凉透气、束腰健身的独特效能，使用方便，男女皆宜，具有很高的使用价值和较好的保健作用。

张元杰自少年时期便开始向父母学习编织牛筋腰带。首先学习了单边、双边两种花型比较简单的牛筋腰带编织方法，逐步掌握了牛筋腰带基本的生产技艺，后来又向父亲张庆洪学习并掌握了原材料的生产技术。在此基础上，张元杰还积极向赵延修等其他老编织艺人拜师学艺，先后掌握了菊花、一条龙、金钱花等传统花型的编织方法。1992 年，他开始在聊城市印染厂从事管理工作。2002 年，他注册成立聊城市圣帝御封牛筋腰带厂。

张元杰通过对牛筋腰带传统着色工艺的改进，克服了该产品过硬及易脱色的缺陷，掌握了使牛筋腰带着色牢固和手感软硬适度的技术工艺，并申请了该项生产技术工艺的专利。他还在牛筋腰带花型方面进行探索和创新，创制出“五龙带”和“满天星”两种独特的新花型，丰富了牛筋腰带的花型品种。

多年来，张元杰十分注重技艺的传承，培养了张亚文、史延昌、宋海霞若干生产技术骨干，为牛筋腰带这一传统民间手工制作工艺的传承和发展做出了贡献。他的腰带厂还吸收了一批下岗失业人员和残疾人，被评为聊城市就业再就业优秀个人和助残先进个人。2008 年，张元杰被聊城市团委推荐为中国青年创业国际计划导师。

Zhang Yuanjie—
Inheritor of Liaocheng Ox Tendon Belt Craft

Zhang Yuanjie, male, was born in Liaocheng, Shandong Province in 1964.

Ox tendon belt, also known as "cool belt", is one of the exclusive traditional pure handwork folk crafts in Dongchangfu District. This product is made from high-quality ox hide and tendon in west Shandong, by the traditional craft, through a dozen processes, such as material selection, scraping, skinning, water immersion, knitting, shaping, polishing, painting, brazing, etc. It is famous for its delicate patterns and beautiful colors. It is uniquely refreshing, breathable, waist girdling, and bodybuilding. Convenient for use and suitable for both men and women, it has high use value and good health care function.

Zhang Yuanjie began to learn how to knit an ox tendon belt from his parents when he was a teenager. Firstly, he learned the easier single-sided and double-sided knitting methods, and gradually mastered the basic craft of ox tendon belt. Later, he learned from his father Zhang Qinghong and mastered the processing technology of raw materials. On this basis, Zhang Yuanjie also actively learned from Zhao Yanxiu and other veteran knitting artists, and successively mastered the knitting methods of such traditional patterns as "Chrysanthemum" "One Dragon", and "Jinqian Flower". He began to work in Liaocheng Printing and Dyeing Factory in 1992. In 2002, he registered and founded Liaocheng Shengdi Imperial Seal Ox Tendon Belt Factory.

Zhang Yuanjie improved the traditional coloring craft of the ox tendon belt, and overcame the defects of over-hardness and easy decolorization of the product. He mastered the production technology of the ox tendon belt which keeps the color firm and the hardness medium, and applied for the patent of the production technology. He also explored and innovated the pattern of the belt, created two unique new patterns of "Five Dragon Belt" and "Babysbreath", which enriched the variety.

Over the years, Zhang Yuanjie has attached great importance to the inheritance of the craft, trained several production technology backbones such as Zhang Yawen, Shi Yanchang and Song Haixia, etc. He has contributed to the inheritance and development of the traditional folk handicraft of ox tendon belt. His belt factory has also absorbed a number of laid-off unemployed and disabled people, and he has been rated among excellent individuals for employment and re-employment in Liaocheng and voted as the advanced individual for helping the disabled. In 2008, Zhang Yuanjie was recommended by Liaocheng Youth League Committee as a mentor of China Youth Entrepreneurship International Plan.

曲阜琉璃瓦制作技艺传承人——朱玉海

朱玉海，男，1963 年出生，山东曲阜人。

曲阜琉璃瓦制作技艺是中国传统烧制技艺的代表，其选材讲究，制作精细，烧制过程严格，制作流程复杂，制造技艺严谨，并配以各种特殊辅料挂釉烧变，具有其他烧制工艺所不具备的技艺特征。曲阜琉璃瓦制作技艺采用朱氏传统工艺，其系列品种主要有宝顶、大吻、屋兽人物、方脊、沟头滴水、连砖等 100 多种。

朱玉海生于琉璃瓦制作世家，祖籍山西洪洞，祖辈主要从事琉璃瓦档、殿脊、翘檐上的琉璃飞禽瑞兽等工艺品的烧制。明朝洪武三年（1370 年），他们外迁至曲阜城西的兴隆庄（今大庄），负责孔府、孔庙的扩建与修缮工作。他作为朱氏窑户第十二代传人，自幼受到父辈的熏陶，对瓦坯制作等工艺进行了学习，20 世纪 80 年代进入曲阜大庄琉璃瓦厂参加工作。

在专供“三孔”的黄、绿两个传统颜色琉璃瓦的基础上，朱玉海通过理论研究和大量实验，研制出多种新的色系，并加入各种辅助原料，使瓦釉色彩更加纯正。他在实际生产过程中通过不断创新，结合各种高科技检测、计量仪器，保持了琉璃瓦制作工艺的先进性，解决了很多琉璃瓦制作技艺机械化、现代化过程中出现的问题。同时，他还掌握了陶瓷、壁画等其他各种色釉，扩展了色釉技术的使用范围，对色釉技术的发展起到了一定的作用。

作为琉璃瓦制作的工程师，朱玉海掌握了琉璃瓦制作过程中一系列的核心工艺及创新技术，并对朱氏琉璃瓦的传承历史和技艺的发展进行了深入的研究，为琉璃瓦产业的发展、琉璃瓦制作技艺的延续与传承贡献了一份力量。1995 年，朱玉海被评为“曲阜市劳动模范”。2007 年，他获得“曲阜市民间艺人”的称号。

Zhu Yuhai—Inheritor of Qufu Glazed Tile Craft

Zhu Yuhai, male, was born in Qufu, Shandong Province, in 1963.

Qufu Glazed Tile craft is representative of traditional Chinese firing technology. Its materials are carefully selected, the production is fine, and the firing process is strict. The production process is complicated, requiring rigorous technology. It has the unique technical characteristics. Qufu Glazed Tile craft adopts Zhu's traditional craftsmanship. It has more than 100 series of varieties such as Treasure Dome, Big Kiss, House Beast Characters, Square Ridge, Ditch Edge Dripping Water, Continuous Bricks, etc.

Zhu Yuhai was born in a family of glazed tile craft. His ancestral home is in Hongdong County, Shanxi Province. His ancestors were mainly engaged in the firing of glazed tiles, palace ridges, glazed birds and animals on the eaves. In the third year of the Hongwu Reign of the Ming Dynasty, the family moved to Xinglongzhuang (now called Dazhuang) in the west of Qufu City to take charge of the expansion and renovation of Confucius Mansion and Confucian Temple. As the twelfth generation of descendants of Zhu's kiln household, he was influenced by his father generation and studied tile making and other techniques from his early childhood. In the 1980s, he entered Dazhuang Glazed Tile Factory in Qufu to work.

On the basis of special yellow and green glazed tiles with three holes, Zhu Yuhai developed a variety of new color systems through theoretical research and a large number of experiments, and he added various auxiliary materials to make the glaze color purer. Through continuous innovation in the actual production process, combined with various high-tech testing and measuring instruments, he maintained the advanced technology of glazed tile production, and solved the problems in the process of mechanization and modernization of glazed tile production technology. Meanwhile, he has a certain mastery of other kinds of glazes, such as ceramics, murals, etc. It expands the application scope of the glaze technology and plays a certain role in the development of the glaze technology.

As an engineer of glazed tile making, Zhu Yuhai has mastered a series of core craft and innovative technologies in the process of glazed tile making, and has made a thorough study on the inheritance history and the development of Zhu's glazed tile craft. He has contributed a lot to the development of the glazed tile industry and the continuation and inheritance of the glazed tile craft. Zhu Yuhai was awarded "Qufu Model Labor" in 1995 and "Qufu Folk Artist" in 2007.

兰陵美酒传统酿造技艺传承人——刘剀

刘剀，男，1970 年出生，山东兰陵人，国家级评酒委员，临沂市首席技师。

兰陵美酒生产历史悠久，是北方黄酒传统酿造工艺的典型代表。此酒的琥珀光泽在陈酿中天然生就，郁金香味在微生物代谢中自然天成，色、香、味均有别于普通黄酒的典型风格。经现代科学鉴定，兰陵美酒中含有人体必需的 18 种氨基酸、6 种维生素、11 种微量元素，是一种具有养血补肾、舒筋健脑、益寿强身功能的滋补酒。

刘剀自 1993 年从无锡轻工业学院发酵系毕业后就进入山东兰陵美酒股份有限公司美酒车间工作，师承当时的美酒酿造技艺传承人吕金山，此后一直从事兰陵美酒酿造及其工艺研究工作。1998 年 4 月，刘剀任美酒酿造车间主任，2003 年 9 月晋升为高级工程师。

多年来，刘剀专心学习、潜心研究、踏实实践，在继承兰陵美酒传统酿造技艺的基础上，对兰陵美酒酿造用曲、检验、操作等进行了一定改良，取得了大量研究成果。他探索新技术应用于传统美酒生产过程，利用冷冻除浊和硅藻土过滤、膜过滤技术，解决了传统美酒保质期内混浊沉淀问题。同时对美酒酿造用麦曲、酒母进行培养分离，筛选出适合的菌种制备纯种麦曲和纯种酵母，减少了自然麦曲用量，使兰陵美酒口感得到改善且出酒率大大提高。此外，他还自行设计改进美酒的杀菌设备，通过延长保温时间达到彻底杀菌的目的，使兰陵美酒的酿造技术得以创新发展。

刘剀在主持兰陵美酒生产、管理和研发的同时，还利用专业和技艺特长，组织本公司职工开展兰陵美酒酿造工艺技能培训，培养兰陵美酒生产技术骨干 20 余人；利用果露酒品评特长，为企业培养多名黄、露酒品评人才（其中省级果露酒评酒委员一名）。刘剀通过传承与创新相结合的方式为兰陵美酒传统酿造技艺的发展做出了贡献。

Liu Qi—
Inheritor of Lanling Wine Traditional Brewing Craft

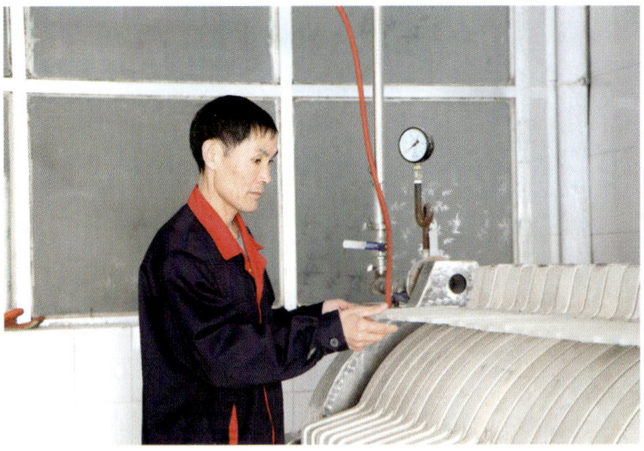

Liu Qi, male, born in Lanling, Shandong Province in 1970, is a state-level wine judge and chief technician of Linyi City.

Lanling Wine has a long history and is a typical representative of the traditional brewing technology of northern yellow rice wine. The amber luster of this wine is natural in aging. The tulip flavor is natural in microbial metabolism. The color, aroma and taste of this wine are different from the typical style of ordinary yellow rice wine. According to modern scientific identification, Lanling Wine contains 18 kinds of amino acids, 6 kinds of vitamins and 11 kinds of trace elements which are essential for human body. It is a nourishing wine with functions of nourishing blood, tonifying kidney, relaxing the mind and strengthening the body.

Since graduating from the Fermentation Department of Wuxi Institute of Light Industry in 1993, Liu Qi has been working in the wine workshop of Shandong Lanling Wine Co., Ltd. and has been engaged in the fine wine brewing and technological research since then under the guidance of his master Lü Jinshan, the then fine wine brewing craft inheritor. In April 1998, Liu Qi was appointed the director of the wine brewing workshop, and was promoted to the senior engineer in September 2003.

Over the years, Liu Qi has devoted himself to dedicated study and steady practice. On the basis of inheriting the traditional brewing craft of Lanling Wine, he has improved the koji, test and operation in making Lanling Wine, and achieved a lot of research results. He explored the application of new technologies in the production of traditional wine, and he solved the problems of turbidity and precipitation during the shelf life of traditional wine by the methods of freezing to remove turbidity, diatomite filtration and membrane filtration. In addition, the fermentation of wheat starter and winemaker was carried out, and suitable strains were screened to prepare pure wheat starter and pure yeast, which reduced the amount of natural wheat starter, improved the taste of Lanling wine and greatly increased the yield of wine. In addition, he also designed and improved the sterilization equipment of wine on his own. Through prolonging the holding time to achieve the purpose of thorough sterilization, the brewing technology of Lanling wine was innovated and developed.

While presiding over the production, management and R & D of Lanling Wine, Liu Qi made use of his major and advantages in craft in colorful ways. He organized the staff of the company to carry out the technical training of Lanling Wine brewing, and he trained more than 20 technical backbones. He also trained many talents of yellow wine and dew wine evaluation for enterprises (including one commissioner of the provincial fruit dew wine evaluation committee). Liu Qi's combination of inheritance and innovation has contributed to the development of Lanling Wine traditional brewing craft.

长岛砣矶砚雕刻技艺传承人——王守双

王守双，男，1941年出生，山东长岛人，山东省工艺美术大师、中国文房四宝制砚艺术大师。

砣矶砚是鲁砚的代表之一，其砚雕技艺是山东传统雕刻技术的重要组成部分。长岛砣矶砚的制研工序主要分为采料、构思、雕刻、打磨、上蜡等。砣矶砚雕工细腻精美，意境开阔，设计巧妙，图案稳中有变，纹理层次分明，风格沉着淳朴，体现了长岛深厚的文化底蕴。

王守双自幼酷爱书法绘画、雕刻艺术，常常跟随父亲王启良到磨石嘴村山崖下的砚坑中采砚石，认真学习雕刻技艺。他深知要想在砚石上刻出漂亮的字，首先要练好书法。因此，他在书法、绘画的练习上下足了工夫。1979年，王守双创办了砣矶砚工艺美术社，开发了砣矶金星雪浪砚和山水石盆景两种产品。多年来，他创作设计的砣矶砚成功出口美国、日本、韩国等国家和地区。

王守双的雕工细腻精美，意境开阔，极富感染力。他在制砚时常因料行意，利用天然石纹和铜屑的自然排布巧妙截取，顺势走刀，在砚池中制造出万千意象，再随着砚材的天然形态雕上流云、修竹、幽兰，镌上行草真隶，使一方方砣矶砚或粗犷朴拙，或典雅精妙，构思、格调、造型、工艺等皆达到了较高的艺术品位，十分惹人喜爱。

王守双的作品《书魂砚Ⅰ》在2008年的中国国际艺术博览会上荣获银奖。2009年，其作品《托起明天的太阳砚》在“首届中国北方旅游商品创新设计大赛”中荣获金奖。2010年，王守双参加中国民间工艺品博览会，作品《书魂砚Ⅱ》获金奖。为了更好地保护和传承砣矶砚雕刻技艺，王守双向来自省内外学习砣矶砚雕刻技术的数十人传授技艺。此外，他还积极组织砚雕艺人召开座谈会，到中小学给学生讲解砣矶砚知识，为长岛砣矶砚雕刻技艺的传承发展做出了贡献。

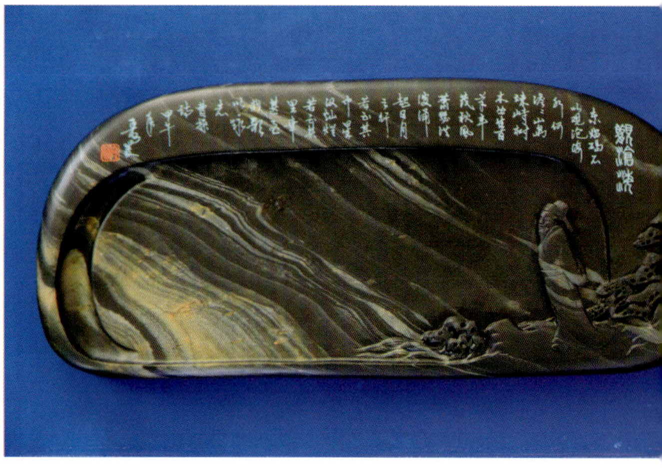

Wang Shoushuang—Inheritor of Changdao Tuoji Inkstone Carving Skills

Wang Shoushuang, male, born in 1941, is from Changdao County, Shandong Province. He is a master of arts and crafts in Shandong Province.

Tuoji Inkstone is one of the representatives of Shandong inkstone. Its carving skills are an important part of Shandong traditional carving technology. The production process of Changdao Tuoji Inkstone mainly covers material collection, conception, sculpture, polishing, waxing and so on. Tuoji Inkstone carving is exquisite, broad-minded, ingenious in design, stable and changeable in pattern, distinct in texture and simple in style, reflecting the profound cultural heritage of Changdao County.

Wang Shoushuang has been fond of calligraphy, painting and sculpture since his childhood. He often followed his father Wang Qiliang to collect inkstones in the inkstone pit under the cliff of Moshizui Village, and earnestly studied the sculpture skills. He knows that in order to engrave beautiful characters on inkstones, he must first practice calligraphy. Therefore, he has made great efforts in the practice of calligraphy and painting. In 1979, Wang Shoushuang founded the Tuoji Inkstone Arts and Crafts Society and developed such two kinds of products as "Tuoji Shiny Wave Inkstones" and "Miniature Mountain Landscapes". Over the years, his Tuoji inkstones have been successfully exported to the United States, Japan, South Korea and other countries.

Wang Shoushuang's sculptures are exquisite and elegant, with a broad artistic conception and great appeal. In making inkstones, he often used natural stone patterns and copper scraps to cleverly intercept and follow the trend to create thousands of images in the inkstone pond. Based on the natural form of inkstone, he carved up floating clouds, tall bamboos, orchid and grass, adds characters in Xin or Cao style, making the inkstone rough and simple, or elegant and delicate. The design, style, shape and craft all reach a higher level of art, which is very cute and popular.

Wang Shoushuang's masterpiece *Book Soul Inkstone* I won the silver prize at the 2008 China International Art Exposition. In 2009, his work *The Sun Inkstone Welcoming Tomorrow* won the gold medal in the first North China Tourist Commodity Innovation Design Competition. In 2010, Wang Shoushuang participated in the China Folk Crafts Exposition and won the gold prize for his work *Book Soul Inkstone* II. In order to better protect and inherit the Tuoji Inkstone carving skills, Wang Shoushuang has taught ten artists from inside and outside the province. In addition, he actively organized Tuoji Inkstone carving artists to hold symposiums, and went to primary and secondary schools to introduce Tuoji Inkstone to the students, contributing to the inheritance and development of Changdao Tuoji Inkstone carving skills.

东昌澄泥烧制技艺传承人——郭太星

郭太星，男，1973年出生，山东聊城人。

澄泥制品是中国古代文人流传的一种纯手工艺术形式，具有鲜明的地域特征和浓厚的人文气息。东昌澄泥烧制技艺风格独特、稚拙质朴，具有原生态的文化品格，反映了一定时期的民间文化生活状况。其制品看似碧玉，莹耀生辉；抚如童肌，细润柔滑；叩之有金石之声，铿锵悦耳；用则腻而不滑，贮水不涸，历冰不寒。

郭姓祖先作为澄泥技术的主导，烧制技艺代代相传。郭太星年幼时便跟随祖父郭思亮学习制作澄泥的各道工序。后来，他又在祖辈制作工艺的基础上，四处拜师学艺，经名家指导，刻苦钻研，重新制作澄泥艺术品。1992年，郭太星进入东昌府区澄泥文化艺术有限公司工作至今。

郭太星所制作的东昌澄浆玉泥工艺品用多次澄浆的黄河泥塑形，经过取土、碾碎、制浆、滤泥、澄泥、制坯、晾坯、磨制、雕刻、烧制、药煮等10余道工序纯手工制作而成。根据制作工艺和烧制时间的不同，可制作出橘子红、玫瑰紫、鳝鱼黄、蟹壳青、墨玉黑、斑鸠灰、绿豆砂等不同颜色。郭太星不仅擅长制作砚台，还制作了蟋蟀养罐、文房文玩、活字印模、家居器皿等多个系列艺术品，其窑变极品真正体现了世间独一无二的极品艺术价值。郭太星的刀法利索、简练，制作出的澄泥作品无不胎体细腻、雕刻规整，形成了自己简洁大气的艺术风格。

2010年，郭太星的作品在济南首届中国非物质文化遗产博览会上展出。2012年，其作品在台儿庄第二届中国非物质文化遗产博览会上展出。2013年，其作品参加了山东省陶艺陶瓷精品展。在做好澄泥艺术品的同时，郭太星还十分注重这一技艺的传承与发展。2010年，他参加市级“非遗”进校园活动，在聊城大学与大学生进行“非遗”交流，被聘为客座教授。2011年，他筹备农村青少年“非遗”素质教育基地，力图为东昌澄泥烧制技艺增加新的生命力。

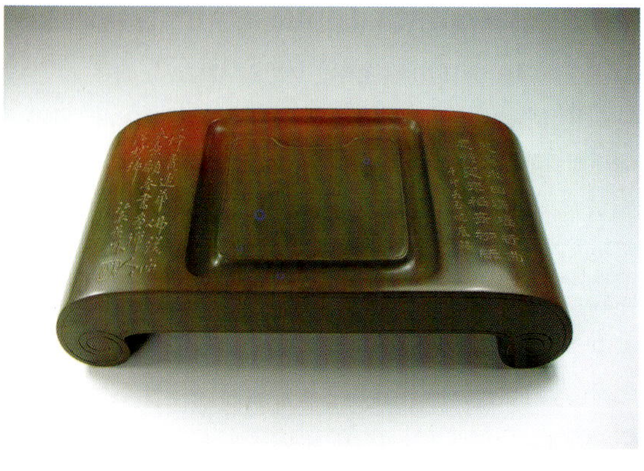

Guo Taixing—Inheritor of Dongchang Chengni Firing Technique

Guo Taixing, male, born in 1973, is a native of Liaocheng, Shandong.

Chengni products are a form of purely handmade artworks popular among ancient literati and scholars of China, with strong regional characteristics and cultural elements. Dongchang Chengni firing technique features a unique and simple style and an original cultural quality, reflecting the folk cultural life of a certain period. Chengni products shine like jade, feel as tender and smooth as the skin of a baby, and give out a sonorous and ear-pleasing sound like metal and stone when knocked. Being smooth but not slippery, Chengni products can be used to contain water and ice.

Guo's ancestors have pioneered in Chengni craftsmanship and passed down the firing techniques from generation to generation. Since his childhood, Guo Taixing has been taught by his grandfather Guo Siliang the production processes of Chengni products. Afterwards, he has absorbed techniques from different craftsmen and worked hard to innovate the production techniques of Chengni artworks. In 1992, Guo Taixing was employed by Dongchangfu District Chengni Cultural Art Co., Ltd. and has worked there thenceforth.

The Chengni artworks produced by Guo Taixing are made of Yellow River mud which has been purified many times through dozens of processes such as getting earth, grinding earth, preparation of slurry, filtering of mud, settlement of mud, production of base, airing of base, polishing, carving, firing and boiling with medicine. With different production methods and lengths of firing, different colors can be produced such as orange red, rose purple, eel yellow, crust green, marble black, dove gray, mung bean sand. Guo Taixing is not only good at producing ink-stones, but also can produce several series of artworks such as cricket boxes, articles for amusement, movable type printing mould and household utensils. His fambe masterworks embody unrivalled artistic values in the world. His cutting techniques are neat and simple. His Chengni works feature an exquisite base, regular carving and a simple and concise artistic style.

In 2010, his works were exhibited in the first China Intangible Cultural Heritage Exposition held in Jinan, Shandong. In 2012, his works were exhibited in the second China Intangible Cultural Heritage Expo held in Taierzhuang, Zaozhuang. In 2013, his works were displayed in the provincial exhibition of selective ceramic crafts. While producing Chengni artworks, he tries to carry on and develop Chengni production techniques. In 2010, he participated in a municipal program of introducing intangible cultural heritage into campuses and was invited as a visiting professor to discuss intangible cultural heritage with the students in Liaocheng University. In 2011, he prepared for the establishment of an Intangible Cultural Heritage Education Base for Rural Teenagers, with an aim to infuse new vigor into Dongchang Chengni firing technique.

枣庄砂陶烧制技艺传承人——项云芳

项云芳，女，1967 年出生，山东枣庄人。

枣庄砂陶烧制工艺大致分为选料、踩泥、制坯、阴干、入窑、烘烧等十几道程序，而其中选料、制坯、阴干、烘烧四道工序尤为重要。枣庄砂陶的主要原料有黏土和煤灰渣，原料晒干后碾磨成粉，按 1:1 的配比搅拌成泥，放置一段时间备用。枣庄砂陶的主要产品包括粗砂壶、大砂缸、砂盆、罐、坛、油灯、油瓶、酒壶等日常生活用品。

项云芳的父亲项守付和母亲李金荣都是砂陶烧制技艺的守护者，两人成婚后创立了当时枣庄最大规模的家族私营陶窑厂。因此，项云芳自幼便得到家庭的艺术熏陶和父母的言传身教，至今从事陶艺工作 20 余年。1989~1999 年，她在枣庄市国营陶瓷一厂从事陶瓷制作和车间管理工作；1999 年在原有的家族陶窑厂基础上，创立枣庄齐村砂陶大作坊。

项云芳主要从事砂陶器的设计和制作，擅长手工制陶。她制陶时注重造型的整体效果和作品内涵，技法独到细腻，具有浓厚的原始神韵和地方特色。此外，她还配合家传的制陶技艺，采用独有的素烧三遍使之产生窑变的烧制技法，使陶品的色彩、质感都与众不同，从而形成了厚重典雅，重气求神的作品风格，并兼顾欣赏性和实用性。

项云芳始终秉承“在保护中传承，在传承中发展”的宗旨，从 2005 年至今，代表省、市、区参加山东省文化产业博览会、中国非物质文化遗产博览会、中国西部博览会、中国国际旅游商品博览会、鲁台经贸洽谈会等大型活动 30 余次。2005 年其作品“船型酒器”“金瓶梅”和“新疆仿皮囊”酒瓶，被中外酒瓶博物馆收藏。2012 年 9 月，她的《美人壶》等两项陶艺作品获国家版权局颁发的著作权证书。项云芳近年来还与齐村镇中学、齐村乔屯联校和齐鲁工业大学等学校合作，建立学生艺术实践基地，为学校和社会各界提供传习的平台和场所，为枣庄砂陶烧制培养后继人才。

Xiang Yunfang—Inheritor of Zaozhuang Sand Pottery Firing Technique

Xiang Yunfang, female, born in 1967, is a native of Zaozhuang, Shandong.

Zaozhuang Sand Pottery firing technique roughly comprises dozens of processes, such as selection of materials, stamping on mud, production of base, drying in the shade, putting into the kiln and firing, of which the selection of materials, production of base, drying in the shade and firing are particularly important. The main raw materials are clay and coal ash slag. After the raw materials get dried, they are ground into powder and mixed with a ratio of 1 : 1 to make mud, which is then placed for a while for later use. The main products of Zaozhuang Sand Pottery are daily necessities such as coarse sand pot, large sand vat, sand basin, tank, jar, oil lamp, oil bottle and wine pot.

Her father Xiang Shoufu and mother Li Jinrong are both protectors of the sand pottery firing technique. After they got married, they established the largest family-owned pottery factory in Zaozhuang at that time. Therefore, from her childhood, Xiang Yunfang has been exposed to art edification of the family and teaching from her parents. So far, she has engaged in the career of ceramic art for more than 20 years. From 1989 to 1999, she worked in Zaozhuang No.1 State-owned Ceramics Factory, responsible for production of ceramics and workshop management. In 1999, on the basis of the family-owned pottery factory, she established a sand pottery workshop in Qicun Town of Zaozhuang.

She is mainly engaged in designing and production of sand pottery wares and good at handmade ceramics. In the production of ceramics, she paid attention to the overall effects of modeling and the connotation of works. Her techniques are exquisite and unique, displaying rich originality and local flavors. Besides, on the basis of the ceramics craft passed down by her family, she applied a unique firing technique to create an effect of fambe by firing the works plainly for three times. The products made with this technique feature unique colors and texture, a dignified and elegant style and ornamental and pragmatic effects.

She has always adhered to the tenet of "carrying on the craft in protection and developing the craft in inheritance". Since 2005, she has participated in more than 30 large-scale activities on behalf of the province, city and district, such as Shandong Cultural Industry Exposition, China Intangible Cultural Heritage Exposition, Western China International Fair, China International Tourist Commodity Fair, Shandong-Taiwan Economic and Trade Fair. In 2005, her works *Ship-shaped Drinking Vessel*, *Gold Wine Bottle* and *Xinjiang Fake Leather Bag* were collected by the Museum of Chinese and Foreign Wine Bottles. In September 2012, her two ceramic works including *Beauty Pot* got copyright certificates from the National Copyright Administration. These years, she has also cooperated with schools such as Qicun Town Middle School, Qicun Qiaotun Joint School and Qilu University of Technology, providing schools and all quarters of the society with a platform and venue for learning and practicing and cultivating talents to carry on the Zaozhuang Sand Pottery firing technique.

博山琉璃烧制技艺传承人——孙即杰

孙即杰，男，1945 年出生，山东淄博人，中国玻璃艺术大师。

博山的琉璃生产始于汉代，到元末已形成大规模生产。琉璃属于硅酸盐系列，琉璃产品大多属于工艺观赏品，其中花瓶、摆件、花球品种繁多，水果、动物等品种造型逼真，晶莹剔透，栩栩如生。中华人民共和国成立后，博山成立专门生产琉璃的厂家——博山美术琉璃厂，并建立了研发中心等机构。

孙即杰自幼跟随父亲学习琉璃制作。1960 年，进入博山美术琉璃厂工作；1985 年，担任博山美术琉璃厂工艺美术研究所所长，全面系统地研究琉璃文化和工艺；1992 年，担任博山美术琉璃厂总工艺美术师，负责全厂琉璃生产的技术和制作工艺；1993 年，同日资成立淄博爱美工艺品有限公司，兼任总经理；2003 年企业改制后成立淄博爱美琉璃制造有限公司，担任董事长、艺术总监。

孙即杰恢复了难度极大的琉璃名贵色料“鸡油黄”的生产技艺，生产出纯正的鸡油黄，还制作出琉璃名贵料器金红、鸡肝石、绿松石等，使得这些名贵色料得以传承。花球是博山琉璃中的重要产品，孙即杰在继承传统花球制作技艺的基础上不断创新，使花球的花色品种达百余种。多年来其个人设计的大量琉璃作品，富有地方特色，形成了典雅蕴籍的个人艺术风格。

几十年来，孙即杰广泛传授技艺，培养人才，有 12 名学生获得山东省工艺美术大师及其他荣誉称号。

2008 年，孙即杰的琉璃作品古韵瓶、古墩瓶获得香港首届紫荆花杯国际文化艺术博览会金奖，并于同年被英国皇家珍宝博物馆收藏。2009 年，他的作品彩釉系列花瓶获得第 35 届山东省陶瓷琉璃艺术创新评比金奖。在 2012 年举办的中国工艺美术博览会上，其大型琉璃作品“天籁之韵”被评为金奖。在 2012 年“博山杯”中国陶瓷琉璃艺术大奖赛上，其琉璃作品“福禄”获金奖。

Sun Jijie—Inheritor of Boshan Colored Glaze Firing Technique

Sun Jijie, male, born in 1945, is a native of Zibo, Shandong and a master of glass art in China.

The colored glaze production of Boshan dates back to the Han Dynasty. By the end of the Yuan Dynasty, large-scale production emerged. Colored glaze is classified under the silicate series. Most colored glaze products are used as ornaments. There are a variety of colored glaze products, such as vases, ornaments and flower globes. Colored glaze products can take the shapes of fruits, animals, etc., which are crystal and lifelike. After the People's Republic of China was founded, a special factory of colored glaze was established in Boshan—Boshan Colored Glaze Art Factory, along with organizations such as R&D Center.

Since his childhood, Sun Jijie has learned the production of colored glaze from his father. In 1960, he entered Boshan Colored Glaze Art Factory. In 1985, he served as the head of the arts and crafts research institute of Boshan Colored Glaze Art Factory, carrying out comprehensive and systematic researches on colored glaze culture and crafts. In 1992, he served as the chief industrial artist of Boshan Colored Glaze Art Factory, taking charge of the production techniques of colored glaze. In 1993, he established a joint venture, Zibo Aimei Handiwork Co., Ltd. and served as its general manager. In 2003, the enterprise was restructured into Zibo Aimei Colored Glaze Manufacture Co., Ltd., in which he served as the chairman of the board and the art director.

Sun Jijie has restored the production technique of "chicken oil yellow", a precious pigment of colored glaze, which is extremely difficult. He has produced pure "chicken oil yellow" and other precious pigments such as golden red, chicken liver stone and turquoise, so that these precious pigments can be carried on. Flower globes are an important product among the colored glaze products of Boshan. He has made innovation while carrying on the conventional production techniques of flower globes to create hundreds of designs. For years, a lot of his colored glaze works have demonstrated rich local flavors and an elegant artistic style.

For decades, Sun Jijie has spread his techniques widely and cultivated many talents. 12 students of his have won honorary titles, such as "The Craft Master of Shandong Province".

In 2008, the ancient style bottle and vase, two colored glaze works of Sun Jijie, won the gold award in the first Hong Kong Bauhinia Cup International Culture and Arts Exposition and were collected by British Royal Treasure Museum in the same year. In 2009, his series colored ceramic glaze vases won the gold award in the thirty-fifth Appraisal of Ceramic Glaze Art Innovation of Shandong Province. In the China Arts and Crafts Exposition 2012, his large colored glaze work *Heavenly Charm* won the gold award. In 2012, in the "Boshan Cup" Competition of Chinese Ceramic Glaze Art, his colored glaze work *Blessing* won the gold award.

石榴盆景栽培技艺传承人——肖元奎

肖元奎，男，1948年出生，山东枣庄人，山东省盆景艺术师。

石榴盆景是从石榴“盆栽”演变而来，峄城民间石榴盆景艺术起源于清代，至今已有200多年历史。当地拥有著名的石榴园林——冠世榴园，原材料丰富。厚重的文化底蕴和丰富的自然资源激发了峄城民间艺人的创作激情，他们制作的石榴盆景风格独特，外形优美，被誉为“无声的诗，立体的画，活的雕塑”。

肖元奎的父亲生前酷爱草木花卉、果木盆景，对石榴盆景更是尤为钟爱，有着自己独特的石榴盆景栽植、制作、管理、养护经验。受家庭环境影响，肖元奎自幼喜爱石榴盆景，在遵循传统制作方法的前提下，不断探索、构思、创造，形成了独树一帜的艺术风格。

肖氏石榴盆景尤其注重古桩石榴的养护管理，巧妙运用古桩枯干的“舍利干”制作，以蟠扎为主，修剪与蟠扎相结合，使盆景增加美感，提高了观赏效果。作品除具有一般盆景缩龙成寸、小中见大、师法自然的艺术风格外，还具有苍老奇特、古朴野趣、刚柔相济的特征。肖元奎制作的盆景表现出了鲁南人的豪爽气质和峄城冠世榴园的恢宏气势。通过长期的实践，肖元奎用修剪时废弃的粗壮石榴树干，通过培根催芽等技术手段，探索出了培养石榴盆景的新方法。通过这种方法培养出的盆栽造型奇特，成型较快，有效节约了石榴资源。

保护不忘传承，肖元奎之子肖长胜在父亲的悉心传授下，已掌握一套成熟的石榴盆景栽培技艺。肖元奎也不断将盆栽技艺传播出去，现任峄城区石榴盆景艺术协会会长，有石榴盆景作品1000余件，其中近百件获得国家、省市盆景展大奖，其石榴盆景栽培基地——峄城石榴盆景悦心园已接待海内外游客数万人。

Xiao Yuankui—Inheritor of Pomegranate Bonsai Cultivation Techniques

Xiao Yuankui, male, born in 1948, is a native of Zaozhuang, Shandong, and a bonsai artist of Shandong Province.

Pomegranate bonsai has evolved from pomegranate "potted landscape". The folk pomegranate bonsai art of Yicheng can date back to the Qing Dynasty and has a history of more than 200 years. There is a famous pomegranate garden—World-famous Pomegranate Garden in Yicheng, which is abundant in raw materials. The folk artists of Yicheng have been inspired by the profound cultural deposits and rich natural resources, who have created pomegranate bonsai works with a unique style and a beautiful appearance, which are honored as "silent poems, stereoscopic pictures, and living sculptures".

The father of Xiao Yuankui was fond of bonsai of flowers, plants and fruit trees and particularly loved pomegranate bonsai, and had unique experience in the cultivation, production and maintenance of pomegranate bonsai. Influenced by the family, Xiao fell in love with pomegranate bonsai in his childhood. While following the conventional production method, he has developed a special artistic style through ceaseless exploration, conception and creation.

Xiao emphasizes the maintenance and management of pomegranate trees with an old stub and makes a clever use of "Sheligan" production with old stub and dry trunk to enhance the aesthetic and ornamental effect of bonsai. Based on curling and combining it with trimming, the works not only display artistic styles such as displaying essence in limited space, embodying much in little and following the natural law which can be found in common bonsai, but also show characteristics such as antique and uniqueness, primitive simplicity and combination of hardness and softness. The bonsai produced by Xiao Yuankui reflects the generous temperament of the people of Southern Shandong and the grand vigor of the World-famous Pomegranate Garden of Yicheng. Through long-term practice, Xiao Yuankui has explored a new method to cultivate pomegranate bonsai with the thick and solid pomegranate trunk abandoned when trimming the trees and applying technologies such as cultivating roots and accelerating germination. The bonsai cultivated with this method features a unique appearance, takes a shape quickly and thus effectively saves pomegranate resources.

Xiao Yuankui has devoted himself to the protection and inheritance of pomegranate bonsai cultivation techniques. Under his careful instruction, his son, Xiao Yuansheng, has mastered a set of mature cultivating techniques. He keeps spreading the bonsai cultivation techniques and now serves as the president of Yicheng Pomegranate Bonsai Art Association. He has over 1,000 pomegranate bonsai works, of which nearly a hundred have won awards in national, provincial and municipal bonsai exhibitions. His pomegranate bonsai cultivation base—Yicheng Pomegranate Bonsai Garden, has received tens of thousands of tourists from home and abroad.

即墨老酒黄酒传统酿造技艺传承人——韩吉臣

韩吉臣，男，1965年出生，山东即墨人，高级酿酒师、品酒师。

山东即墨黄酒厂是以姜介甫“源聚兴”老酒馆为基础，沿用传统工艺生产黍米黄酒，并将其产品正式定名为“即墨老酒”。从此，“即墨老酒”成为山东即墨黄酒厂的代表产品。即墨老酒在传承传统酿造工艺精髓的基础上，运用“煮饭加糗糜”的独特工艺，在中国黄酒行业中独树一帜。以传统工艺酿制的即墨老酒，酒色纯正，红褐晶莹，焦香馥郁，醇厚适口，以口味独特、营养丰富闻名于世，被誉为“液体蛋糕”“营养酒王”。

1987年，韩吉臣从青岛第一轻工业学校发酵专业毕业后，分配到山东即墨黄酒厂，学习酿酒工艺。在工作中其自身酿酒水平逐步提高，2003年成为黄酒厂总工程师。任职期间，他组织带领技术人员开发了即墨清酒、即墨花雕等系列产品。

在开发系列产品过程中，韩吉臣在继承“古遗六法”传统工艺的基础上，对酿造工艺进行了改进。他研究的低温发酵法、分罐发酵法、槽式发酵法，使即墨老酒的品质得到了极大提升。韩吉臣从即墨老酒特有工艺制作的陈伏麦曲中分离出优良健壮的纯种酵母，优中选优，培育出的“一株黍米酿酒酵母及应用”获国家发明专利。将此专利应用于生产中后，酒的口味更加清爽，鲜度、香气更加突出。其改进的泡烫米工艺，让米充分吸水，缩短了糊化、糖化时间，节约了能源，使酒质更加完美，酒体更加协调，风格典型性更加突出，达到色、香、味的更高标准。

韩吉臣凭借自己多年的工作经验，每年都会举办培训班，目前已培训骨干人才100余人，让他们真正掌握即墨黄酒传统酿造工艺，使这一传统技艺不断得到传承。

Han Jichen—Inheritor of Jimo Traditional Brewing Technique of Yellow Rice Wine

Han Jichen, male, born in 1965, is a native of Jimo, Shandong and a senior winemaker and taster.

Shandong Jimo Yellow Rice Winery produces millet wine with traditional process on the basis of "Yuanjuxing" Old Pub owned by Jiang Jiefu. Its product was officially named as "Jimo Laojiu". From then on, "Jimo Laojiu" has become a typical product of Shandong Jimo Yellow Rice Winery. Carrying on the essence of traditional brewing process, it has applied the unique process of "adding millet into cooked rice" and developed a style of its own in the yellow rice wine industry of China. Jimo Laojiu features a pure color of crystal reddish brown, a strong scorch smell and a mellow taste. It is world-famous for its unique flavor and rich nutrition and has been reputed as "liquid cake" and "king of nutritious wines".

In 1987, after Han Jichen graduated from the major of fermentation in Qingdao No. 1 Light Industry School, he was dispatched to Shandong Jimo Yellow Rice Winery to learn brewing technique. Through practicing, he improved his brewing technique gradually. In 2003, he became the chief engineer of the yellow rice winery. During his term of office, he led other technicians to develop a series of products such as Jimo Sake and Jimo Huadiao.

While inheriting the "six ancient brewing requirements", he has improved the brewing process. The low temperature fermentation method, fermentation in different tanks, groove fermentation method studied by him have significantly improved the quality of Jimo Yellow Rice Wine. Han has separated good and strong pure yeasts from the aged wheat yeasts produced with the unique process of Jimo Laojiu. After selecting the best from the best, he has developed a "millet brewing yeast and its application" and won a national invention patent. After the patent is applied in the production, the flavor of the yellow rice wine is more refreshing, with more prominent freshness and bouquet. The rice soaking process improved by him makes rice fully absorb moisture, shortens the time of gelanitization and saccharification, saves energy, which perfects the vinosity and makes the wine body more balanced, highlights the typical style and fulfills the best standard of color, bouquet and flavor.

With rich working experience, he organizes training classes every year and has trained over 100 backbone talents and enabled them to truly master the traditional brewing process of Jimo Yellow Rice Wine, and pass on the traditional technique.

妙府黄酒传统酿造技艺传承人——于秦峰

于秦峰，男，1962年出生，山东即墨人，全国轻工行业劳动模范、中国酿酒大师、山东省首席技师。

妙府黄酒传统酿造技艺是在传统即墨老酒的基础上发展演变而来的，其技艺的核心是“糗糜法”。糗糜法的基本要领是“古酿六法”，亦称“古遗六法”，即“黍米必齐，曲糵必时，水泉必香，陶器必良，湛炽必洁，火齐必得”。在传统工艺的基础上，妙府黄酒有着自己独特的生产方法，酿造出的黄酒具有酒色纯正、焦香馥郁的特点。

于秦峰善于学习和创新。1979~1982年，于秦峰在山东即墨黄酒厂酿酒车间先后做过烧火工、糖化工、榨酒工、制曲工、酵母工，跟随师傅张廷智较系统地学习了酒曲、酿造等工艺。1993年，于秦峰调离即墨黄酒厂，进入山东即墨妙府老酒有限公司工作，任总酿酒师、总工程师。在于秦峰的带领下，妙府老酒全面继承和发扬了即墨老酒传统酿造工艺的精髓，并不断创新。

在全面继承妙府黄酒传统酿造技艺的基础上，于秦峰围绕即墨传统老酒的特点，先后研制了十几种创新的老酒产品，其中功能性老酒获得国家发明专利。于秦峰还和很多大专院校进行了产、学、研的合作，经过几年的科技创新和工艺改进，即墨妙府老酒的制作方法获得中国国际专利与名牌博览会金奖，共获得各类专利19项，妙府老酒也因此被授予“中国历史文化名酒”“山东名牌和山东省著名商标”等称号。

于秦峰积极开展传承保护活动，已带徒弟130余人，培养出了一批优秀的黄酒酿造高技能人才。于秦峰还专门成立了“黄酒酿酒技术研发小组”，亲自担任组长，科研成果显著，为妙府黄酒传统酿造技艺的传承做出了重要贡献。

Yu Qinfeng—Inheritor of the Traditional Brewing Technique of Miaofu Yellow Rice Wine

Yu Qinfeng, male, born in 1962, is a native of Jimo, Shandong, a model worker of the national light industry, a brewing master of China and a chief technician of Shandong Province.

The traditional brewing technique of Miaofu Yellow Rice Wine has evolved from that of "Jimo Laojiu", the core of which is "cooked millet method". The essentials of the method are "six ancient brewing requirements", namely, "the millet used must be full and tidy, the yeasts must be made at the right time, the water must be sweet and refreshing mineral water, the containers must be good, utensils must be sterilized, the duration and degree of heating must be appropriate". On the basis of traditional technique, the production method of Miaofu Yellow Rice Wine is unique. The yellow rice wine produced with this method features a pure color and a thick scorch bouquet.

Yu Qinfeng is good at learning and innovation. From 1979 to 1982, he worked as a burning worker, a saccharifying worker, a winepress worker, a starter propagation worker and a yeast worker and learned the systematic techniques of yeast production and brewing, etc., from his master Zhang Tingzhi. In 1993, he was transferred from Jimo Yellow Rice Winery to Shandong Jimo Miaofu Laojiu Co., Ltd. and worked as the chief brewer and engineer. Under his leadership, "Miaofu Laojiu" carried on the essence of traditional brewing technique of "Jimo Laojiu" and kept pursuing innovation.

While carrying on the traditional brewing techniques of Miaofu Yellow Rice Wine, Yu has developed dozens of innovative yellow rice wines based on "Jimo Laojiu", of which the functional yellow rice wine has won a national invention patent. He has established an industry-academy-research cooperation with colleges and universities, in which the traditional brewing technique was studied deeply. After years of scientific innovation and process improvement, the production method of Jimo "Miaofu Laojiu" has won a gold award in the China International Patent & Brand Exposition, and won 19 patents. For this reason, "Miaofu Laojiu" has won other honors such as "The Historical and Cultural Wine of China", "The Famous Brand of Shandong and a Famous Trademark of Shandong".

He has made active efforts in protection and inheritance. He has tutored over 130 disciples and cultivated a batch of excellent and skillful talents for brewing of yellow rice wine. He has established a "R&D team of yellow rice wine brewing technology" and headed the team to make distinctive scientific research achievements, which makes an important contribution to the inheritance of the traditional brewing technique of Miaofu Yellow Rice Wine.

莱芜口镇南肠传统制作技艺传承人——刘锋

刘锋，男，1972年出生，山东莱芜人，莱芜口镇南肠传统制作技艺第六代传承人。

在清道光年间，口镇就是香肠的制作基地。口镇南肠为山东名吃之一。口镇南肠是在百年生产历史的基础上，精选当地新鲜猪肉，汲取口镇之水，加之传统配方，天然露晒而成。而今口镇南肠已成为莱芜街头巷尾家喻户晓的知名品牌。

1993 年 3 月，刘锋到莱芜市顺香斋南肠厂工作，在酱菜车间当学徒。1995 年，他开始师从第五代口镇南肠传承人李广清，学习莱芜南肠的加工与制作。时至 2004 年 3 月，因国企改制，企业宣布破产，刘锋购得老厂土地使用权，带领企业老职工和技术骨干重新整合，迅速恢复生产，使南肠工艺得到了传承和发展。

工作期间，刘锋精心研究口镇南肠的百年制作技艺，熟练掌握了口镇南肠的刮肠、原料配比、拌馅、灌装、晾晒及蒸煮六大技艺。从原料配方到加工环节，刘锋结合现代生产方式进行细致的科学分析，寻求和多家科学院校合作，使口镇南肠的制作技艺不断提升，在继承传统技艺的基础上，研制开发了多种口味的新产品，受到了市场的青睐。在刘锋的努力下，口镇南肠被评为“莱芜名吃”“山东名吃”“山东食品业十佳消费品牌”和“山东著名品牌”等。

为保护这一传统技艺，刘锋积极开展传承活动，培养后继人才，现已收徒 3 人。同时，他广泛开展各种形式的技术培训和传授，成立专门的技艺传习所和研究所，积极整理口镇南肠百年发展史上的一些传统工艺、配料方法，使莱芜口镇南肠代代相传。刘锋本人也获得了相关部门的认可，被评为“山东省农业产业化发展突出贡献个人”。

Liu Feng—Inheritor of Traditional Production Technique of Laiwu Kouzhen Sausage

Liu Feng, male, born in 1972, is a native of Laiwu, Shandong and the sixth generation inheritor of the traditional production technique of Laiwu Kouzhen sausage.

During the Daoguang Reign of the Qing Dynasty, Kouzhen Town was a production base of sausage. Kouzhen Sausage is one of the famous snacks of Shandong. Kouzhen sausage is produced by exposure to the natural sunlight and made of selective fresh local pork and water of the town with the traditional formula. Today Kouzhen Sausage has become a famous brand well-known to all households in Laiwu.

In March 1993, Liu Feng joined Laiwu Shunxiangzhai Sausage Factory as an apprentice in a workshop of pickles. In 1995, he began to learn from Li Guangqing, the fifth generation inheritor of Kouzhen Sausage, the processing and production of Laiwu Sausage. By March 2004, the state-owned enterprise was restructured, so the enterprise was declared bankrupt. Liu Feng purchased the land use right of the former factory. He led former workers and technical backbones of the former enterprise to reincorporate and restore production quickly. As a result, the production process of sausage was inherited and developed.

Mr. Liu has devoted himself to the research of the century-long production techniques of Kouzhen Sausage, and became familiar with six techniques of sausage production including cleaning, proportioning of raw materials, mixing the stuffing, filling and steaming. From the formula of raw materials to the processing steps, Mr. Liu has made a detailed scientific analysis based on the modern production methods and sought after cooperation with different scientific institutions and schools to keep improving the production techniques of Kouzhen Sausage. While carrying on the traditional technique, he has also developed several new products with different flavors, which are popular in the market. Under his effort, the products have won many honors such as "The Famous Snack of Shandong" "The Famous Snack of Laiwu" "Top Ten Best Consumption Brands in the Food Sector of Shandong" and "The Famous Brand of Shandong".

To protect the traditional technique, Mr. Liu has launched programs to cultivate talents actively. Now he has accepted three disciples and made a prominent contribution to the inheritance and development of Laiwu Kouzhen Sausage. Meanwhile, he has launched various technique training and teaching programs and established a specifilized institute for the learning and practice of techniques and researches. He has actively organized some traditional techniques and formula in the century-long development history of Kouzhen Sausage. As a result, Kouzhen Sausage has been infused with vigor and passed down from generation to generation. He has been recognized by related departments and been honored as "The Individual with a Prominent Contribution to the Industrialization of Agriculture of Shandong Province".

亓氏酱香源肉食酱制技艺传承人——亓飞

亓飞，男，1973年出生，山东莱芜人，亓氏酱香源肉食酱制技艺第七代传承人。

亓氏酱香源肉食酱制技艺起源于清道光年间，迄今已有100多年历史。亓氏酱香源传统技艺源自宫廷，后在民间不断改进创新，融进了民间市井口味，成为脍炙人口的百姓菜肴。其制作食品种类繁多，有酱鸡、酱牛肉、酱猪肉、酱肠等十几个品种，制作出的酱肉色泽鲜艳，入口柔绵，肥而不腻，是莱芜地区首屈一指的地方名吃。

亓飞自幼跟随祖父学习酱肉制作技艺，几十年来，熟悉掌握了祖传酱肉的制作方法。1991年，亓飞在父亲的帮助下正式开办了“亓氏酱香源店”，后逐渐做大做强；2001年，他成立莱芜亓氏酱香源食品有限公司，扩大生产规模，产品远销到北京、济南、青岛等地；2011年，其公司改名为山东省亓氏酱香源食品有限公司，亓飞担任董事长兼总经理，挑起了亓氏酱香源肉食酱制技艺传承的大梁。

在继承亓氏酱香源肉食酱制传统技艺的基础上，亓飞将传统技艺与现代工艺进行结合，生产出了口味更加纯正、质量更加安全的食品，制作的酱肉已达16个品种，产品香而不腻，享誉四方。2010年10月，亓飞的酱香系列参加了“中国首届非遗博览会”和“山东文化产业博览会”，获得了消费者的一致好评，提高了产品的知名度。

为保护这一传统技艺，亓飞积极开展传承活动，开办了亓氏酱香源博物馆，同时不忘培养后继人才。在传承的同时，亓飞也积极将这一传统技艺传播出去。他多次参加国家、省、市的一系列公益性救助、资助活动，提高品牌的社会责任感和知名度。2013年5月，亓飞被共青团山东省委、山东青年联合会授予“山东省五四青年奖章”。

Qi Fei—
Inheritor of Production Technique of Jiangxiangyuan Sauced Meat of Family Qi

Qi Fei, male, born in 1973, is a native of Laiwu, Shandong and the seventh generation inheritor of the production technique of Jiangxiangyuan Sauced Meat of Family Qi.

The production technique of Sauced Meat of Family Qi dates back to the Daoguang Reign of the Qing Dynasty and has a history of more than a century. Originating from the imperial court, the production technique has been improved and innovated by folks and blended with the folk flavors. It has become popular among the folks. There are dozens of kinds of sauced meat such as sauced chicken, sauced beef, sauced pork and sauced intestines. The sauced meat is freshly bright, tastes soft, fat but not greasy and has become one of the most popular local snack of Laiwu.

Since his childhood, Qi Fei has learned the production technique of sauced meat from his grandfather. For decades, he has skillfully mastered the production method of sauced meat passed down from his ancestors. In 1991, with the help of his father, he opened Family Qi's Jiangxiangyuan Store, which grew in size and strength later. In 2001, he established Laiwu Family Qi's Jiangxiangyuan Food Co., Ltd., expanded the production and sold products to different regions such as Beijing, Jinan and Qingdao. In 2011, the company was renamed as Shandong Family Qi's Jiangxiangyuan Food Co., Ltd. Qi Fei served as the chairman of the board and general manager, taking the main responsibility of carrying on the sauced meat of Family Qi's Jiangxiangyuan.

To protect the technique, Qi's Fei has actively held inheritance activities, opened a Family Qi's Jiangxiangyuan Museum and cultivated talents. Besides, he has also tried to spread the traditional technique. He has participated in a series of public-benefit helping activities of the state, province and city to enhance the social responsibility and fame of the brand. In May 2013, Qi Fei was awarded "The May 4 Youth Medal of Shandong Province".

隆盛糕点制作技艺传承人——脱安利

脱安利，男，1963年出生，山东青州人，隆盛糕点制作技艺第六代传承人。

青州作为多民族居住的古城，是山东东部主要的回族聚居区。回族丰富的饮食文化经过多年的沉淀，形成了众多味美可口、风格独特的食品，隆盛糕点在其中久负盛名。其采用传统技艺和独特配方精工细作而成，具有入口即化、油而不腻的特点。

脱安利于1979~1993年在益都阀门厂工作期间，利用业余时间从事隆盛糕点的制作。1993年从工作单位辞职后，脱安利把全部精力放在了学习隆盛糕点制作上，全面继承了从精选原材料、糕点配方到工艺流程，再到经营方法等全套生产经营秘诀。

脱安利在传承传统技艺的同时，对蛋糕的部分工艺进行了优化，使产品质量得到了提高，同时对蒸熟面的工艺进行了改进，提高了产品质量和效率。在脱安利的带领下，隆盛糕点先后被山东省工商局评定为“山东省著名商标”，被潍坊市评定为“潍坊风味名吃”。另外，脱安利协助山东省非物质文化遗产研究中心完成了“青州隆盛糕点传统制作技艺研究”课题，对隆盛糕点的文化、工艺、工具等进行了详细记录，并将其列入“山东省老字号文化遗产重点项目”。

2003年，脱安利开始带徒弟传授隆盛糕点制作技艺，目前已传授徒弟57人。由于隆盛糕点在制作过程中坚守传统工艺，生产过程中的质量控制要靠多年积累的经验，且生产工艺复杂，较难掌握，脱安利经常手把手教学，用其学习时得出的经验来教授徒弟，并多次协助中央电视台、山东电视台、《大众日报》、《山东工商教育报》等资深媒体对隆盛糕点传统技艺进行报道，提高了隆盛糕点的知名度，为隆盛糕点的传承做出了重要贡献。

Tuo Anli—Inheritor of Production Technique of Longsheng Pastry

Tuo Anli, male, born in 1963, is a native of Qingzhou, Shandong and the sixth generation inheritor of the production technique of Longsheng Pastry.

As an ancient city inhabited by several nationalities, Qingzhou is a main settlement of Hui people in the east of Shandong Province. The rich food culture of Hui people, after years of accumulation, has formed many palatable and unique foods. Longsheng Pastry has enjoyed a good reputation for long, which is produced with fine workmanship, traditional techniques and unique formula, and melts in mouth and tastes fat but not greasy.

When Tuo Anli worked in Yidu Valve Factory from 1979 to 1993, he spent his spare time in the production of Longsheng Pastry. After he quit from his workplace in 1993, Tuo Anli devoted all his energy to learning the production of Longsheng Pastry. He has fully inherited the complete set of production and operation recipes ranging from selection of raw materials, pastry formula to the process flow and then to the operating methods.

While inheriting the traditional technique, he has optimized some processes of cakes and improved the product quality. He has also improved the process of steaming flour and enhanced the product quality and efficiency. Under his leadership, Longsheng Pastry has been honored as "The Famous Trademark of Shandong Province" by the Industry and Commerce Administration of Shandong Province and honored as "The Famous Snack of Weifang" by Weifang City. He has assisted the Intangible Cultural Heritage Research Center of Shandong Province to finish the research program on "The Traditional Production Technique of Qingzhou Longsheng Pastry", made detailed records of the culture, process and tools, etc. of Longsheng Pastry, which has been listed among the major time-honored cultural heritage projects of Shandong Province.

In 2003, he began to teach the production technique of Longsheng Pastry to his apprentices. So far, he has had seven disciples and tutored them item by item from selection of materials and formula to production processess. Since no additive is added in the production of Longsheng Pastry, the quality control relies on experience accumulated over the years. In addition, its production process is complex and difficult. He often teaches his apprentices step by step based on his own experience. He has assisted the mass media such as CCTV, Shandong TV, *Public Daily* and *Shandong Industry, Business and Education Newspaper* in their reports of the traditional technique of Longsheng Pastry. By doing so, he has enhanced the popularity of Longsheng Pastry and made an important contribution to the inheritance of Longsheng Pastry.

泰山驴油火烧制作技艺传承人——李鹏

李鹏，男，1974年出生，山东泰安人，泰山驴油火烧第七代传承人。

泰山驴油火烧历史悠久，作为泰山旅游文化的重要元素，是泰山食文化的重要内容之一。因出锅后的泰山驴油火烧外酥里嫩，色、形、味俱佳，且宜于存放，便于携带，受到很多人的喜爱，成为地方名吃。

李家泰山驴油火烧以家传的方式进行传承，有据可考的传承自清仁宗嘉庆年间开始，到李鹏这一辈已传承七代，历经了200多年。随着老一代传承人的谢世，特别是家族后代在职业选择上发生的变化，鲜有人继承这一技艺，出现了后继乏人的危机。李鹏为了发掘、传承、保护和发展这一技艺，在2005年注册了以泰山驴油火烧为主打产品的泰安红豆开元贸易有限公司，扩大生产规模，保护这一遗产。

李鹏在传承百年秘方的基础上也创新了泰山驴油火烧的发展模式，完善了工艺制作流程，着重提升产品品质，引入了现代化生产设备。2009年，泰山驴油火烧专用炉“电热式食品烤烙箱”获国家专利，被“中国北交会”评为“金奖特色旅游产品”，家传家具用具与现代化设备的结合保证了产品的质量和口感，使越来越多的人认识泰山驴油火烧。在李鹏的努力下，泰山驴油火烧于2010年作为“特供指定产品”成功进入上海世博会，“泰山火烧专用烤烙箱”及“泰山火烧工艺六法”成功通过泰安市科学技术局成果鉴定，作为“特邀非遗项目”参加了“首届中国非物质文化遗产博览会”并取得可喜成绩。泰山驴油火烧被山东省工商联授予“山东历史名吃”称号。

李鹏积极培养后继人才，将这一传统技艺传承下去。因贡献突出，先后获得“第三届山东省优秀进城创业青年”“第九届泰安市青年科技奖”“好客山东服务金牌”等荣誉称号。

Li Peng—Inheritor of Production Technique of Taishan Donkey Oil Burger

Li Peng, male, born in 1974, is a native of Tai'an, Shandong and the seventh generation inheritor of Taishan Donkey Oil Burger.

Taishan Donkey Oil Burger has a long history. As an important element of the tourism culture of Mount Tai, it is an important part of Mount Tai food culture. Taishan Donkey Oil Burger is crispy outside but tender inside, and tempting in color, appearance and taste, easy for storage and portable. Therefore, it is popular among many people and has become a famous local snack.

Family Li's Taishan Donkey Oil Burger has been passed down from generation to generation, which can date back to the Jiaqing Reign of the Qing Dynasty according to historical records. It has been passed down for seven generations for more than 200 years when Li Peng inherited it. It met a crisis of no qualified inheritor for various reasons until Li Peng took this responsibility. In order to explore, inherit, protect and develop the technique, Li Peng registered Tai'an Red Bean Kaiyuan Trade Co., Ltd. based on Taishan Donkey Oil Burger, expanding the production scale to protect the cultural heritage.

On the basis of inheriting the century-lasting recipe, he has innovated the inheritance and development model of Taishan Donkey Oil Burger, perfected the production process, improved the product quality and introduced modern production equipment. In 2009, the specialized oven for Taishan Donkey Oil Burger, "electrically Heating Food Oven" won the national patent and honored as the "Gold Award Winning Special Tourism Product" in the North China Tourism Fair. The combination of furniture and utensils passed down by the family and modern equipment guarantees the quality and taste of products and make more and more people fall in love with Taishan Donkey Oil Burger. Under his efforts, Taishan Donkey Oil Burger was introduced into Shanghai World Exposition as a "Specially Designated Product" in 2000. The specialized oven for Taishan Donkey Oil Burger and the six-step process of Taishan Donkey Oil Burger passed the appraisal of Office of Science and Technology of Tai'an. As "The Specially Invited Intangible Cultural Heritage Project", it made gratifying achievements in The First China Intangible Cultural Heritage Exposition. Taishan Donkey Oil Burger has been awarded "The Famous Historical Snack of Shandong Province" by the Federation of Industry and Commerce of Shandong.

Li Peng has tried to cultivate talents with an aim to carry on the traditional technique. For his prominent contribution, he has won honorary titles in succession such as "The Third Excellent Young Entrepreneurs of Shandong Province" "The Ninth Tai'an Science and Technology Award for Youth", and "The Gold Medal for Service in Friendly Shandong".

邹平酸浆豆腐制作技艺传承人——孙怀兵

孙怀兵，男，1975 年出生，山东邹平人，邹平酸浆豆腐制作技艺传人。

西董镇位于邹平县南部山区，用酸浆点豆腐是当地流传了上千年的豆腐加工方法。酸浆是指制作豆腐后沥出的汁水在温度适宜的情况下，由自身的乳酸菌发酵而成的一种物质。用酸浆点豆腐，辅之当地优质水资源，制作出的酸浆豆腐细腻嫩白，口感香甜，清香爽口。如今虽然豆腐的制作技艺已见诸不少著作，但真正的传统制作技艺仍然像千余年来那样靠师徒之间言传身教，还要凭悟性和长期实践的经验和感觉才能掌握，难以言表和形成文字。

1993 年，孙怀兵在邹平县读完小学和中学后，转到北京军地专修学院上学。后成立餐饮公司，开始专注研究邹平酸浆豆腐制作技艺，现任北京百福来客餐饮管理有限公司总经理、北京上嘉良品科技发展有限公司董事长。

为传承酸浆豆腐制作这一古老技术，孙怀兵成立了邹平县豆腐文化协会，会员单位已达 201 家。2011 年 9 月，他又在酸浆豆腐发源地西董镇孙家峪村保护及修缮了古老的豆腐坊，保留了原来的石磨及做工用具。同时，孙怀兵还不忘将这一传统技艺传播出去，在北京的“物美大卖场”“金五星市场”等大型超市现场制作孙大嫩酸浆豆腐，得到了当地民众的喜爱，并在国家商标总局注册了“孙大嫩酸浆豆腐”商标，统一了标识，为传承这一古老技艺做出了重要贡献。

2011 年 4 月，孙怀兵在全国开展的最具影响力年度新闻人物推选活动中，获得“中国餐饮管理自主创新十大杰出青年企业家”称号。2012 年，“孙大嫩酸浆豆腐”获得“中国餐饮十大最具影响力诚信品牌”，并获得第七届中国药膳养生技术制作大赛团体金奖。

Sun Huaibing—
Inheritor of the Production Technique of Zouping Sour Pulp Tofu

Sun Huaibing, male, born in 1975, is a native of Zouping, Shandong, and the inheritor of the production technique of Zouping Sour Pulp Tofu.

Xidong Town is located in the southern mountainous region of Zouping County. Adding sour pulp is a method to produce tofu which has been prevailing in the local area for over a thousand years. Sour pulp is a substance coming from the juice released after the production of tofu being fermented by its own lactic acid bacteria under an appropriate temperature. By adding sour pulp into tofu and using the water resources of good quality of local areas, the tofu produced is tender and white, tastes sweet and refreshing. Though the production technique of tofu can be found in many works, the real traditional production technique is passed from the master to apprentices with words and practice for thousands of years and can be mastered only by comprehension and long-term practical experience, because it is difficult to be expressed in words.

In 1993, after graduating from the primary school and middle school, Sun was transferred to Beijing Military College. Later, he established a catering company and began to devote himself to the research of production technique of Zouping Sour Pulp Tofu. Now he serves as the general manager of Beijing Baifu Laike Catering Management Co., Ltd. and chairman of the board of Beijing Shangjia Liangpin Technological Development Co., Ltd.

In order to carry on the ancient production technique of Sour Pulp Tofu, Sun has established Tofu Culture Association of Zouping County, which has admitted 201 member organizations. In September 2011, he protected and repaired the ancient tofu workshop at Sunjiayu Village of Xidong Town, the birthplace of Sour Pulp Tofu and preserved the old stone mill and tools. Meanwhile, he tries to spread the traditional technique by producing Sun Danen Sour Pulp Tofu in large supermarkets of Beijing such as Wu-Mart Hypermarket and Golden Five Stars Market, which became popular among local people. He has registered a trademark of "Sun Danen Sour Pulp Tofu" in the State Administration of Trademarks to unify the identification, which made an important contribution to the inheritance of this ancient technique.

In April 2011, in the selection event of the most influential figures of the year launched nationwide, Sun won an honor of "Ten Best Youth Entrepreneurs for Independent Innovation of Catering Management in China". In 2012, "Sun Danen Sour Pulp Tofu" was honored as "Ten Most Influential Brands of Integrity in the Catering Industry of China" and won a gold award for teams in the seventh China Medicated Food & Health Promotion Competition.

傳承人

〈 山东省省级非物质文化遗产项目 〉
代表性传承人

第四卷

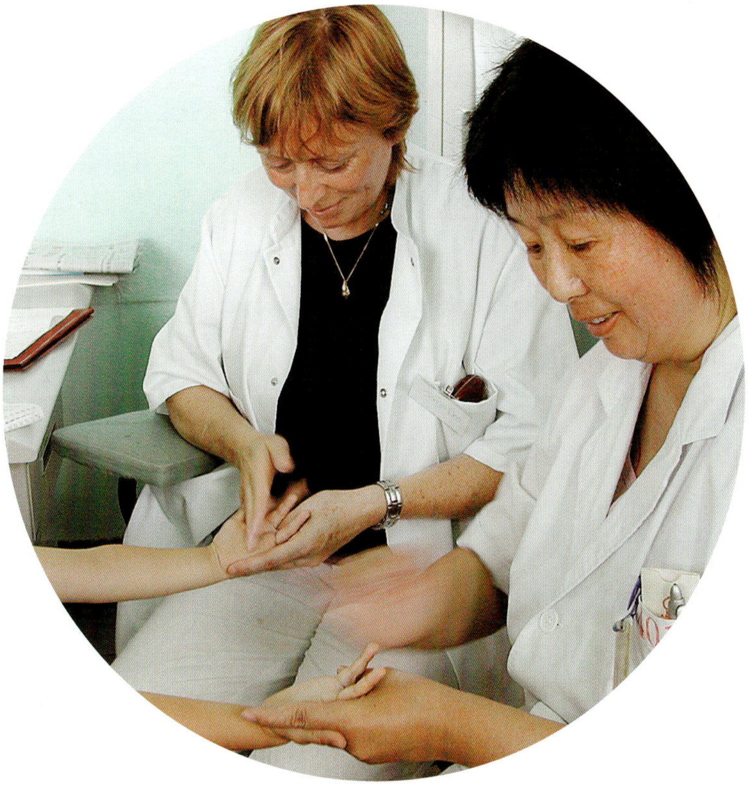

传统医药
Traditional Medicine

扈氏鼻炎膏制作工艺传承人——扈福证

扈福证，男，1981 年出生，山东淄博人。

扈氏鼻炎药膏在民间已经流传了 200 多年，对鼻炎引发的头疼、鼻塞、喘息、流涕等症状，具有很好的治疗作用。扈氏鼻炎药膏在治疗中遵循中医理论，根据肺气不宣发、肺浊气沉积等形成鼻炎的原因，从病根着手，用药膏直接接触病变部位，消炎杀菌，同时通过鼻内腔神经及毛细血管的传导和渗透，引起喷嚏，通过喷嚏反射，将肺内积蓄的浊气毒素迅速排出，达到从根本上治疗鼻炎的目的。扈氏鼻炎药膏是一种较为科学合理的祖传民间医药，具有无创伤、痛苦小、副作用少等优势。

扈福证的父亲扈新立从事鼻炎药膏熬制，扈福证从小耳闻目染，学会了扈氏鼻炎药膏的熬制技艺，成为扈氏鼻炎药膏制作技艺的第八代传人。为继承家族医术，他报考了泰山医学院，系统地学习并掌握医学知识，利用业余时间帮助父亲熬制药膏，给鼻炎患者上药，掌握了一定的鼻炎治疗知识。多年来通过对扈氏鼻炎药膏制作工艺的研究和实践，他掌握了全部的家传配方和熬制技术，并对鼻炎药膏熬制工艺进行了科学改进。

在用药配方上，扈氏鼻炎药膏选用的药物为纯中药，无激素，药性温和，患者对药物没有依赖性。在药膏的熬制上，扈福证熬制的药膏无毒副作用，可直接接触病灶，与内服药相比，减少了对肠胃的刺激，同时减少了忌口对患者带来的不便，不影响患者对营养的正常摄入。治疗方面，扈福证还特制了“U”型鼻塞，这种鼻塞既避免了药塞倒吸入鼻腔内部，又保证了患者呼吸的自由，使患者使用药膏更加方便、安全。

扈氏鼻炎药膏是地方医药文化的杰出代表。2006 年，扈氏鼻炎药膏申请国家发明专利；同年，“U”型鼻塞申请国家外观设计专利。多年来扈福证一直致力于扈氏鼻炎药膏制作工艺的传承与弘扬。

Hu Fuzheng—
Inheritor of Family Hu's Rhinitis Ointment

Hu Fuzheng, male, born in 1981, is a native of Zibo, Shandong.

Family Hu's Rhinitis Ointment has been popular among the folks for over 200 years, which boasts a magic curative effect for symptoms such as headache, nasal obstruction and running nose caused by rhinitis. In its treatment, the ointment obeys the TCM theory, starts from the root causes of rhinitis such as lung "qi" obstruction and accumulation of polluted lung "qi", touches the diseased region directly with the ointment to diminish inflammation and kill bacteria. Through the transmission and infiltration of the nerves and blood capillaries in the nasal cavity, it triggers sneezing and through the sneezing reflex, discharges the polluted and toxic elements out of the lungs quickly, thus curing rhinitis fundamentally. Family Hu's Rhinitis Ointment is a scientific and reasonable folk medicine passed down from ancestors, boasting advantages such as freedom of trauma, little pain and few side effects.

Hu Fuzheng's father, Hu Xinli has been engaged in the production of rhinitis ointment. Therefore, since his childhood, Hu Fuzheng has been influenced by his father and mastered the production technique of Family Hu's Rhinitis Ointment and become the eighth generation inheritor of the production technique of Family Hu's Rhinitis Ointment. In order to inherit the family's medical skill, he signed up for Taishan Medical College and systematically studied and mastered medical knowledge. In his spare time, he also helped his father produce ointment, apply ointment on rhinitis patients and thus has mastered certain knowledge of rhinitis treatment. Through his research and practice of the production technique of Family Hu's Rhinitis Ointment over the years, he has mastered all formula and production techniques passed down by his ancestors and made some scientific improvement to the production technique of rhinitis ointment.

In terms of formula, Family Hu's Rhinitis Ointment selects pure herbal medicine, which is free of hormone and has a mild nature. The patients will not develop drug dependence. The ointment produced by Hu Fuzheng is free of toxic and side effects and can be directly applied to the diseased region to diminish inflammation. Compared with medicine for oral administration, it has reduced the stimulus to the intestines and stomach of patients and the inconvenience caused to the patients for abstaining from certain foods and does not affect the normal absorption of nutrition by the patients. In terms of treatment, Hu Fuzheng has also produced a special "U" shaped device, which can avoid the medicine from sucking back into the naval cavity and guarantee the breathing freedom of the patients. It is safer and more convenient for the patients to use the ointment.

Family Hu's Rhinitis Ointment is an outstanding example of local medical culture. In 2006, it won a national invention patent. In the same year, the "U" shaped device won a national design patent. For years, Hu Fuzheng has been committed to carrying on and spreading the production technique of Family Hu's Rhinitis Ointment.

三字经流派推拿疗法传承人——葛湄菲

葛湄菲，女，1960 年出生，山东青岛人，青岛市中医医院儿科主任，主任医师。

小儿推拿是中医学的重要组成部分，是儿科的一种重要治疗方法。三字经流派推拿疗法属于传统医药的推拿范畴，1877 年由山东牟平人徐谦光创立。徐谦光以三个字为一句话，编著《推拿三字经》，该著作虽未出版，但在民间广为流行。三字经流派推拿疗法历经 100 多年的传承与发展，成为近代小儿推拿疗法中最具有代表性的一个流派。

葛湄菲 1983 年毕业于山东中医学院，后就职于青岛市儿童医院，随后被派往青岛市中医医院儿科学习三字经流派推拿技术。2001 年，她调入青岛市中医医院儿科工作，现任青岛市中医医院儿科主任。

葛湄菲在治疗手法上善用独穴治病，只用一个穴位，多推、久推，以得效为度，这是其他流派所不具备的。她总结出推、揉、捣、拿、分合、运六个推拿常用手法，结合以线形穴位为主的特定穴进行推拿，不仅治疗效果好，还容易学习和掌握。三字经流派创造了推某穴位代替某方剂的独特方法，推拿取穴少而每穴操作时间长，可重复操作，便于临床推广和应用。葛湄菲在工作实践中，建立了疾病前的科普宣教、疾病中的中医治疗、疾病恢复期的保健推拿、体质调理融为一体的综合诊疗模式。多年来她专注于三字经流派推拿技术研究，系统整理总结了三字经流派推拿的学术体系特色与临床技术规范，为三字经流派推拿的规范化推广奠定了基础。

葛湄菲热衷于三字经流派推拿疗法的传承与推广，一直坚持用三字经流派推拿技术治疗小儿常见病，受到人们的广泛认可和学术界的肯定。2008 年，三字经流派小儿推拿临床技术研究通过青岛市科技成果鉴定；2009 年，她的三字经流派推拿文献整理研究获山东中医药科学技术三等奖。三字经流派推拿疗法已进入高等中医药院校的规范教材，为弘扬中华优秀传统中医文化做出了积极的贡献。

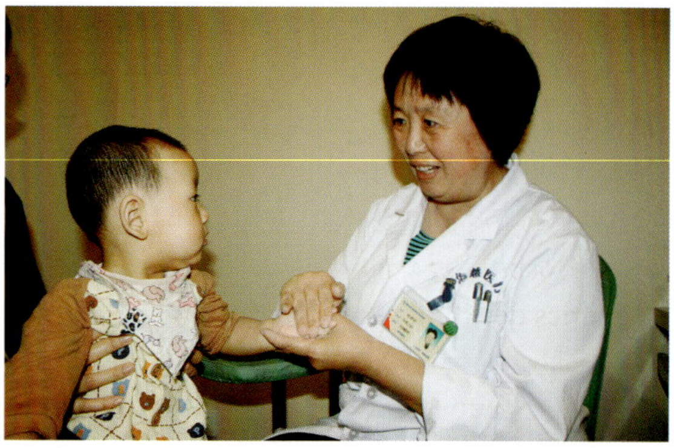

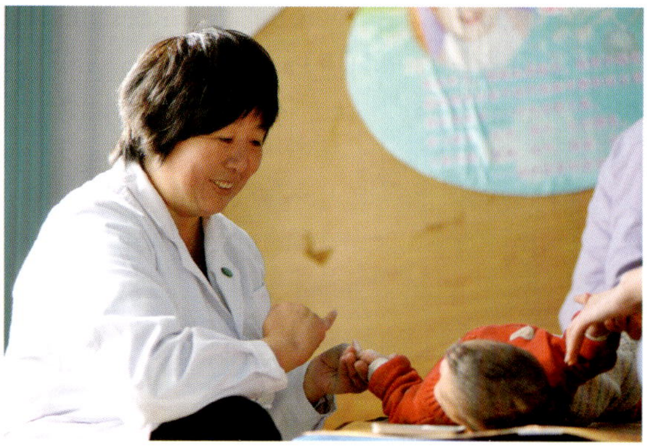

Ge Meifei—Inheritor of Massage Therapy of Three Character Primer School

Ge Meifei, female, born in 1960, is a native of Qingdao, Shandong, the director and chief physician of pediatric department of Qingdao TCM Hospital.

Infantile massage is an important part of TCM as well as an important therapeutic method of pediatrics. The Massage Therapy of Three Character Primer School belongs to the massage category of traditional medicine, which was invented by Xu Qianguang, a native of Mouping, Shandong, in 1877. Xu compiled "Three Character Primer of Massage", which was not published, but was popular among the folks. This school of massage techniques, after being inherited and developed for more than a century, has become a most typical school among the modern infantile massage therapies.

Ge Meifei graduated from Shandong TCM College in 1983 and later worked in Qingdao Children's Hospital. Later, she was dispatched to the pediatric department of Qingdao TCM Hospital to study the Massage Technique of Three Character Primer School. In 2001, she was transferred to the pediatric department of Qingdao TCM Hospital and now serves as director of the pediatrics department of Qingdao TCM Hospital.

Ge Meifei was good at treating diseases with a singular acupuncture point in the therapy. She massaged a singular acupuncture point frequently for long until the effect was achieved, which is not found in other schools. She has summarized six common massage techniques, namely, pushing, kneading, pounding, seizing, splitting and integrating, as well as carrying. She massaged the specific acupuncture points based on linear ones, which not only achieves a good curative effect, but also is easy to learn and master. The school has created a unique method of massaging some acupuncture point instead of using some agents. Few acupoints are covered and the massage time on each acupoint is long, which can be operated repeatedly and is convenient for clinical promotion and application. During her work, Ge Meifei has established a comprehensive diagnosis and treatment model integrating science popularization before falling ill, TCM treatment during the illness, health promoting massage and physical conditioning during the recovery period. For years, she has been committed to the research of the Massage Thergpy of Three Character Primer School, systematically sorted out and summarized the academic system characteristics and clinical operation specifications of the school and laid down a foundation for the regulation of the massage techniques.

Ge Meifei is enthusiastic in carrying on and promoting the massage therapy of Three Character Primer School and has always insisted on treating common pediatric diseases with the massage techniques, and has been widely recognized and accepted by the academic circle. In 2008, her research of clinical technology of infantile massage of the Three Character Primer School passed the appraisal of scientific and technological achievements of Qingdao. In 2009, her literature review research on the Three Character Primer school of massage won a third prize for TCM science and technology of Shandong. The Massage Therapy of Three Character Primer School has been included in the regular teaching materials of TCM colleges and contributed actively to the promotion of the excellent TCM culture of China.

傳承人

山东省省级非物质文化遗产项目
代表性传承人

第四卷

民俗

Folk Customs

淄博花灯会传承人——张向仁

张向仁，男，1949年出生，山东淄博人，淄博市花灯协会会长。

淄博花灯，始于春秋战国，最初叫“号灯”，用于战争中指挥三军，后随着工商业特别是丝绸业、印染业、彩绘业的发展，生产的灯用于观赏，又叫“纱灯”或“灯彩”，至明清时已具有相当规模和较高水平。淄博花灯种类繁多，工艺精湛，特色鲜明。装饰中运用彩绘、剪纸等民间工艺，富有鲜明的地域文化特色。制灯赏灯已成为当地民众普遍喜爱和经常开展的文化活动，并成为一个重要的文化品牌。

张向仁自小就对花灯艺术兴趣浓厚，1967年在山东农药厂参加工作后，受到耿玉新师傅的指点，专心学习芯子灯制作技艺。1976年，他加入厂工会俱乐部专门从事文化工作，致力于民间艺术研究与创作，对花灯制作进行改良，尤其是对芯子灯进行改进，由原来的1人芯子，改为2人芯子，甚至3~5人的多人芯子。张向仁设计的花灯曾多次代表中华人民共和国出国参加“中国花灯展”。1993年，为意大利、巴基斯坦设计花灯共70余台；设计制作的“孔雀开屏”“云影古塔”等大型花灯代表中华人民共和国出访俄罗斯、德国，分别参加在莫斯科和柏林举办的“中国花灯展”；2010~2013年，连续四年负责中国淄博花灯艺术节的组织策划和花灯的设计工作，设计的花灯参观人数达5万人次。

张向仁设计的花灯具有浓厚的地方文化特色，与当地的风俗、故事相结合，比如蒲松龄的聊斋故事、淄博的孝文化故事和当地的民间传说等。百姓在观灯的同时，也能欣赏到发生在身边的历史故事和传说。淄博花灯会成为淄博一张亮丽的文化名片。

张向仁的代表作品获得文化部群文司、山东省文化厅和淄博市人民政府的多种奖项。近年来，他又先后培养了数名技术人才和近百名制灯技术工人，为淄博花灯会这一民俗文化的传承做出了较大贡献。

Zhang Xiangren—Inheritor of Zibo Festive Lantern Fair

Zhang Xiangren, male, was born in 1949, a native of Zibo, Shandong, and chairman of Zibo Festive Lanterns Association.

Zibo Festive Lantern dates back to the Spring and Autumn and Warring States Period, which was at first called "ordering lanterns" and used to command the armies in a war. Later, with the development of industry and commerce, particularly silk industry, printing and dyeing industry and color painting industry, the lanterns were also called "yarn lanterns" or "colored lanterns", which were used for watching and had formed a considerable scale by Ming and Qing Dynasties. There are a variety of Zibo festive lanterns, featuring a fine workmanship and distinctive characteristics. Folk arts such as colored painting and paper-cutting were applied to the decoration of festive lanterns, displaying distinctive regional cultural elements. Production and watching of festive lanterns have become popular cultural activities which are often held by local people and become important cultural brands.

Zhang Xiangren has developed keen interest in festive lanterns since his childhood. In 1967, after he joined Shandong Pesticide Factory, he began to learn the production technique of festive lanterns from his master Geng Yuxin. In 1976, he joined the club of trade union of his factory to engage in the research and creation of folk arts. He improved the production technique of festive lanterns, particularly changing the core of the lantern from one-man to two-man and even to three to five-man. In 1993, he designed over 70 festive lanterns for Italy and Pakistan. The large festive lanterns designed and produced by him such as "Peacock Spreading its Tail" and "Ancient Pagoda under Clouds" were exhibited in Russia and Germany on behalf of China on the Chinese Festive Lantern Shows held in Moscow and Berlin respectively. From 2010 to 2013, he was responsible for organizing Zibo Festive Lantern Art Festival of China. The festive lanterns designed by him were visited by 50,000 persons.

The festive lanterns designed by Zhang Xiangren are rich in local cultural elements by combining with local customs and stories, like the ghost stories of Pu Songling, the filial piety stories of Zibo and other local folk legends, etc. While watching the lanterns, the public can enjoy the historical stories and legends that happened around them. Zibo Festive Lanterns Fair has become a brilliant cultural card of Zibo.

The festive lanterns designed by Zhang Xiangren has been exhibited on China Festive Lantern Shows on behalf of China for many times. His works have won many awards from the Cultural Department of Shandong Province and the People's Government of Zibo City. In recent years, he has cultivated several technicians and nearly a hundred workers of lantern production, making a prominent contribution to the inheritance of Zibo Festive Lantern Fair.

东镇沂山祭仪传承人——张孝友

张孝友，男，1973 年出生，山东临朐人，沂山风景区管委会副主任。

沂山，又名“东泰山”，古称“海岳”“神岳”，素享“五镇之首”之誉，是龙山文化的发源地。东镇沂山祭仪，源于历代帝王对东镇沂山的“望秩之礼”，大禹时期即开始祭祀沂山，自汉至清历代对沂山屡有增封，祀典不废。民国以后，沂山祭仪又以民间祭祀的方式得以传承，传至当代则成为沂山当地群众自发举行的祭祀天地的民俗活动。

张孝友自 2004 年就职于临朐县沂山风景区管理委会以来，一直致力于东镇沂山的历史文化整理和研究，研究课题主要有东镇祭祀文化、碑刻文化、岳镇文化、岳镇海渎祭祀等。同时，他还注重加强对“岳镇海渎祭祀”的史料搜集和实地考察学习，查阅并征集了大量的岳山、镇山、海庙、渎庙，北京天坛、地坛、先农坛、曲阜孔庙等古代祭祀仪式的珍贵史料；先后对全国各大庙坛以及重要的皇家御祭场所进行了实地调研。

张孝友掌握了较丰富的历史知识和古代祭仪知识，为主持祭祀仪式奠定了良好的基础。2005~2011 年，张孝友已连续七届担任“东镇沂山祭仪”的主祭，对沂山祭祀仪式熟记于心，主持严谨，认真有序。他严格按照礼仪程序进行，每一次祭祀活动都能让参与者清晰地看到我国传统文化从古至今发展变化的脉络。

2009 年，张孝友出版了专著《沂山石刻》，并挖掘整理了《沂山祭祀文化》一书。他先后撰写了几十篇沂山文化专题研究文章，系统整理了实物碑刻百余块、碑文数百篇，收集古建构件、饰物等文物百余件。张孝友还参与组织了沂山祭山大典活动，复原祭祀礼仪，参演人数达数万人次，影响广泛，为东镇沂山祭祀文化的活态性传承和保护做出了重要贡献。

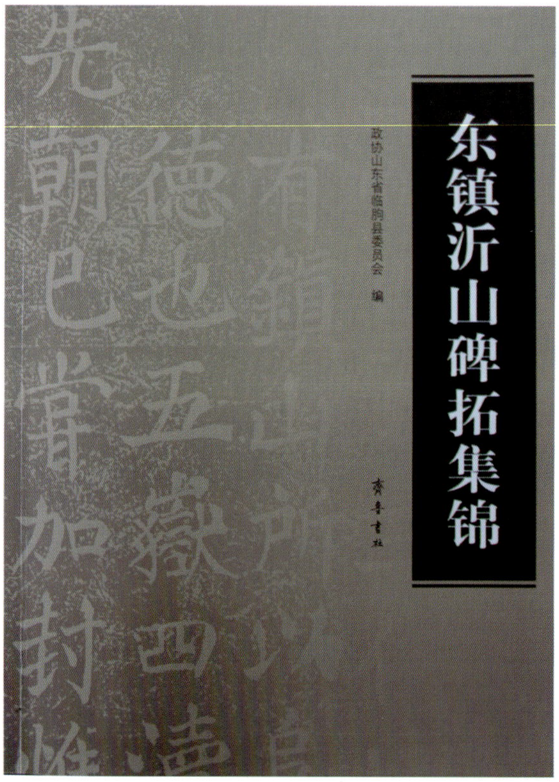

Zhang Xiaoyou—Inheritor of Dongzhen Yishan Sacrificial Ritual

Zhang Xiaoyou, male, was born in 1973, a native of Linqu, Shandong and deputy director of Yishan Scenic Spot Administration Committee.

Yishan, also known as Eastern Taishan, was called "Haiyue" or "Shenyue" in the ancient time, and has always been reputed as the "Top of Five Towns", which is the cradle of Longshan Culture. The Yishan Sacrificial Ritual of Dongzhen Town originates from the worshiping ceremony held by emperors of previous dynasties for Yishan. Yishan was worshipped since the time of Yu the Great. From the Han Dynasty to the Qing Dynasty, Yishan had received different titles and been worshipped. In the modern period, the sacrificial ritual of Yishan was carried on in the form of folk sacrificial ceremony. Now, it has become a folk custom event organized by local people to worship the heaven and earth.

Since Zhang Xiaoyou joined the Administration Committee of Yishan Scenic Spot of Linqu County, he has been studying the history and culture of Yishan. His research topics mainly include the sacrificial culture of Dongzhen, the inscription culture, the Yuezhen culture, the sea worshiping of Yuezhen. Meanwhile, he has collected the historical records of "Yuezhen sea worshiping" and made field inspections and studies, retrieved and gathered a lot of precious historical data on the ancient sacrificial ceremonies such as Yueshan, Zhenshan, the Sea Temple, the Du Temple, the Temple of Heaven, the Temple of Earth, the Temple of God of Agriculture in Beijing and the Temple of Confucius in Qufu. He has made field inspections to the major temples and important royal sacrificial sites allover China.

Zhang Xiaoyou has accumulated rich historical knowledge and knowledge on ancient sacrificial ceremonies, which laid a solid foundation for hosting the sacrificial ritual. From 2005 to 2011, he had served as the chief host of Dongzhen Yishan Sacrificial Ritual for seven times in succession. He was familiar with the sacrificial ceremony and hosted the ceremony in a prudent, careful and orderly manner. In every sacrificial ritual, he enabled the participants to have a clear picture of the development vein of traditional Chinese culture from the ancient to the present.

In 2009, he published *Stone Inscriptions of Yishan* and compiled *Sacrificial Culture of Yishan*. He has written dozens of research papers on Yishan culture, sorted out hundreds of stone inscriptions, and collected hundreds of cultural relics such as components and ornaments of ancient architectures. He has organized the great sacrificial ceremony of Yishan to restore the sacrificial ritual, which was involved tens of thousands of participants. With a wide influence, he has made an important contribution to the inheritance and protection of the sacrificial culture of Yishan, Dongzhen.

附录一

关于公布第四批省级非物质文化遗产项目代表性传承人的通知

各市文广新局、省直文化系统有关单位:

为贯彻《中华人民共和国非物质文化遗产法》、国务院办公厅《关于加强我国非物质文化遗产保护工作的意见》(国办发〔2005〕18号)和《山东省人民政府办公厅关于贯彻国办发〔2005〕18号文件做好我省非物质文化遗产保护工作的通知》(鲁政办发〔2005〕94号)有关精神,省文化厅组织开展了第四批省级非物质文化遗产项目代表性传承人的申报和评审工作。经各地申报、专家评审委员会评审、公示、复议论证等程序,最后确定了胡孝华等71人为山东省第四批省级非物质文化遗产项目代表性传承人,现予以公布。

省级非物质文化遗产项目代表性传承人是非物质文化遗产的重要承载者和传递者,是非物质文化遗产活态传承的代表性人物。各市、各有关部门要认真贯彻“保护为主、抢救第一、合理利用、传承发展”的工作方针,积极落实各项保护措施,鼓励非物质文化遗产代表性传承人开展传习活动,为他们创造良好的传习环境,推动非物质文化遗产传承和发扬，为弘扬齐鲁优秀文化，推动文化大发展大繁荣，建设经济文化强省，做出新的贡献。

特此通知。

山东省文化厅

2014 年 5 月 8 日

山东省第四批省级非物质文化遗产项目代表性传承人名单

（共71人）

民间文学4人

序号	项目编码	项目名称	申报地区或单位	代表性传承人		
				姓名	性别	出生年月
1	I-30	柳毅传说	潍坊市寒亭区	张宝辉	男	1955.7
2	I-41	蒙山传说	蒙阴县	张　莉	女	1975.4
3	I-46	胡峄阳传说	青岛市城阳区	胡孝华	男	1961.2
4	I-47	李左车传说	安丘市	邹学顺	男	1948.9

传统音乐5人

序号	项目编码	项目名称	申报地区或单位	代表性传承人		
				姓名	性别	出生年月
5	3—4	山东古筝乐	菏泽市	祝妍芳	女	1975.8
6	3—8	郯马五大调	郯城县	柏文泰	男	1941.5
7	II-2	鲁西南鼓吹乐	巨野县	陈建斌	男	1967.10
8	II-27	古琴艺术	德州市	庞雨珠	男	1935.2
9	II-27	古琴艺术	济南市	朱子易	男	1938.8

传统舞蹈4人

序号	项目编码	项目名称	申报地区或单位	代表性传承人		
				姓名	性别	出生年月
10	4—4	龙灯扛阁	临沂市河东区	李玉常	男	1953.1
11	III-39	盐垛斗虎	东营市东营区	张良一	男	1955.3
12	III-43	孙斗跑驴	广饶县	孙奎山	男	1946.5
13	III-44	戏灯穿花	栖霞市	马洪贵	男	1952.6

传统戏剧 7 人

序号	项目编码	项目名称	申报地区或单位	代表性传承人		
				姓名	性别	出生年月
14	5—9	柳腔	即墨市	袁　玲	女	1962.8
15	5—10	山东梆子	菏泽市	祝凤臣	女	1968.7
16	5—11	莱芜梆子	莱芜市	李长生	男	1963.3
17	5—14	大弦子戏	菏泽市	李学珍	男	1939.11
18	5—17	四平调	金乡县	刘玉香	女	1964.3
19	5—21	扽腔	博兴县	卞项颂	男	1956.8
20	Ⅳ-3	茂腔	青岛市黄岛区	王淑娴	女	1943.8

曲艺 8 人

序号	项目编码	项目名称	申报地区或单位	代表性传承人		
				姓名	性别	出生年月
21	6—1	山东大鼓	山东省艺术研究院	魏素英	女	1949.8
22	6—2	山东琴书	济南市	魏务良	男	1956.9
23	6—2	山东琴书	济南市	杨　珀	女	1963.1
24	6—2	山东琴书	菏泽市	李巧连	女	1950.1
25	6—2	山东琴书	菏泽市	毕　美	女	1960.10
26	6—3	山东快书	山东省艺术研究院	高洪胜	男	1954.11
27	Ⅴ-2	山东琴书	郓城县	何淑玲	女	1946.10
28	Ⅴ-12	山东渔鼓	汶上县	刘炳金	男	1949.9

传统体育、游艺与杂技 6 人

序号	项目编码	项目名称	申报地区或单位	代表性传承人		
				姓名	性别	出生年月
29	Ⅵ-2	莒县查拳	莒县	庄会升	男	1951.3
30	Ⅵ-4	鸳鸯螳螂拳	青岛市	孙日成	男	1967.5
31	Ⅵ-10	文圣拳	汶上县	宋连洪	男	1953.12
32	Ⅵ-16	佛汉拳	东明县	陈洪元	男	1951.4
33	Ⅵ-24	地龙经拳	高密市	杜文明	男	1956.2
34	Ⅵ-30	武当太乙门	济南市槐荫区	林树基	男	1950.3

传统美术 10 人

序号	项目编码	项目名称	申报地区或单位	代表性传承人		
				姓名	性别	出生年月
35	2—7	东昌葫芦雕刻	聊城市东昌府区	王树峰	男	1983.8
36	2—8	曹州面人	菏泽市牡丹区	李双虎	男	1966.5
37	2—11	聂家庄泥塑	高密市	聂臣希	男	1965.1
38	2—2	苍山泥塑	苍山县	刘福祥	男	1944.10
39	2—18	高密剪纸	高密市	曹兆爱	女	1955.8
40	2—19	烟台剪纸	烟台市	栾淑娟	女	1956.3
41	Ⅶ-8	面塑	济宁市市中区	李　刚	男	1968.12
42	Ⅶ-30	济南面塑	山东工艺美术学院	董凤岐	女	1939.12
43	Ⅶ-32	阳谷木雕	阳谷县	王传成	男	1954.12
44	Ⅶ-40	潍县布玩具	潍坊市寒亭区	孙秀兰	女	1978.2

传统技艺 23 人

序号	项目编码	项目名称	申报地区或单位	代表性传承人		
				姓名	性别	出生年月
45	8—1	潍坊风筝	潍坊市寒亭区	张效东	男	1949.10
46	8—4	鲁西南民间织锦技艺	鄄城县	刘春英	女	1965.4
47	8—9	郓城古筝制作技艺	郓城县	刁兆玉	男	1943.8
48	8—14	柳疃丝绸技艺	昌邑市	魏耀琳	男	1954.4
49	8—17	景芝酒传统酿造技艺	潍坊市	赵德义	男	1967.4
50	9—3	鲁菜烹饪技艺	烟台市	张吉顺	男	1948.11
51	Ⅶ-3	蓝印花布印染技艺	苍出县	相友文	男	1935.12
52	Ⅶ-33	威海锡镶制作技艺	威海市环翠区	谷祖威	男	1944.2
53	Ⅶ-35	聊城牛筋腰带制作技艺	聊城市东昌府区	张元杰	男	1964.10
54	Ⅶ-44	曲阜琉璃瓦制作技艺	曲阜市	朱玉海	男	1963.5
55	Ⅶ-51	兰陵美酒传统酿造技艺	苍山县	刘　剀	男	1970.1
56	Ⅶ-64	长岛砣矶砚雕刻技艺	长岛县	王守双	男	1941.10
57	Ⅶ-67	东昌澄泥烧制技艺	聊城市东昌府区	郭太星	男	1973.4
58	Ⅶ-67	枣庄砂陶烧制技艺	枣庄市市中区	项云芳	女	1967.12
59	Ⅶ-70	博山琉璃烧制技艺	淄博市博山区	孙即杰	男	1945.10

序号	项目编码	项目名称	申报地区或单位	代表性传承人		
				姓名	性别	出生年月
60	Ⅶ-79	石榴盆景栽培技艺	枣庄市峄城区	肖元奎	男	1948.1
61	Ⅶ-80	即墨老酒黄酒传统酿造技艺	青岛市	韩吉臣	男	1965.3
62	Ⅶ-80	妙府黄酒传统酿造技艺	即墨市	于秦峰	男	1962.10
63	Ⅶ-82	莱芜口镇南肠传统制作技艺	莱芜市	刘　锋	男	1972.11
64	Ⅶ-82	亓氏酱香源肉食酱制技艺	莱芜市	亓　飞	男	1973.10
65	Ⅶ-84	隆盛糕点制作技艺	青州市	脱安利	男	1963.1
66	Ⅶ-84	泰山驴油火烧制作技艺	泰安市	李　鹏	男	1974.3
67	Ⅶ-86	邹平酸浆豆腐制作技艺	邹平县	孙怀兵	男	1975.12

传统医药 2 人

序号	项目编码	项目名称	申报地区或单位	代表性传承人		
				姓名	性别	出生年月
68	Ⅸ-4	扈氏鼻炎膏制作工艺	淄博市	扈福证	男	1981.3
69	Ⅸ-9	三字经流派推拿疗法	青岛市	葛湄菲	女	1960.4

民俗 2 人

序号	项目编码	项目名称	申报地区或单位	代表性传承人		
				姓名	性别	出生年月
70	Ⅹ-23	淄博花灯会	淄博市张店区	张向仁	男	1949.8
71	Ⅹ-24	东镇沂山祭仪	临朐县	张孝友	男	1973.9

后记
EPILOGUE

《山东省省级非物质文化遗产项目代表性传承人》是山东省完整系统地介绍省级非遗项目代表性传承人的典籍，也是宣传山东省非物质文化遗产的重要工具书。本书记录着山东省省级非遗项目代表性传承人的基本情况、技艺特征、授徒传承等方面的内容，采用图文并茂、中英文结合的形式，力求达到学术性与艺术性的统一，满足各类读者的需求。

山东省文化和旅游厅领导始终关心本书的编撰与出版工作，并在编撰过程中给予了全力支持，在此表示诚挚谢意。

本书的编纂工作得到了山东省十六地市非遗保护中心及省直文化系统工作人员的大力帮助与支持，他们对本书定稿做了最后的校对工作；本书的英文翻译和出版工作由山东大学出版社完成，在此一并表示感谢。

本书文字资料来源于十六地市省级代表性传承人申报书，书中配图由十六地市非遗中心提供。由于编者水平所限，遗漏、缺憾之处在所难免，恳请读者谅解并给予指正。

The Representative Inheritors of the Provincial Intangible Cultural Heritage Projects of Shandong Province is a complete and systematic introduction to the representative inheritors of intangible cultural heritage projects in Shandong Province, and also an important tool book to promote intangible cultural heritage in Shandong Province. It records the basic information, technical characteristics, apprentice ship and other aspects of the representative inheritors of intangible cultural heritage projects in Shandong Province. It adopts the form of combination of pictures and texts, Chinese and English, and strives to achieve the unity of academic and artistic featuers, to meet the needs of all kinds of readers.

Leaders of Shandong Provincial Department of Culture and Tourism have always been concerned about the compilation and publication of this book, and have given full support in the compilation process, and hereby sincere thanks are extended to them. The compilation of this book has been greatly helped and supported by the intangible cultural heritage protection center of sixteen cities in Shandong Province and the staff of the cultural system directly under the provincial government, who have made the final proofreading work for this book. The English translation and publication of this book were completed by Shandong University Press.

The text and data of this book come from the declaration of the provincial representative inheritors of sixteen cities, and the pictures in the book are provided by the intangible cultural heritage center of sixteen cities. Due to the limited ability of the compilers, omissions and defects are inevitable, and suggestions and corrections are welcomed.

图书在版编目（CIP）数据

山东省省级非物质文化遗产项目代表性传承人．第四卷／李国琳主编．—济南：山东大学出版社，2019.10

ISBN 978-7-5607-6501-3

Ⅰ．①山… Ⅱ．①李… Ⅲ．①非物质文化遗产—民间艺人—生平事迹—山东—现代 Ⅳ．①K825.7

中国版本图书馆CIP数据核字（2019）第259878号

责任编辑：张　瑞　张申华

封面设计：牛　钧

出版发行：山东大学出版社

社　址　山东省济南市山大南路20号

邮　编　250100

电　话　市场部（0531）88363008

经　销：新华书店

印　刷：济南巨丰印刷有限公司

规　格：889毫米×1194毫米　1/16

11.5印张　296千字

版　次：2019年10月第1版

印　次：2019年10月第1次印刷

定　价：280.00元
